THINK LIKE A CONQUEROR:

Lessons from History's Greatest Leaders, Champions, and Heroes

By Peter Hollins,
Author and Researcher at
<u>petehollins.com</u>

Table of Contents

INTRODUCTION — 7

CATHERINE THE GREAT — 14

- SHOWCASE YOUR BRAVERY TO INSPIRE TRUST — 21
- PRACTICE SOFT POWER — 23
- FIND A BALANCE — 27
- DAN'S STORY — 29

KING HAMMURABI — 33

- HOLD YOURSELF TO HIGH STANDARDS — 42
- ORGANIZE YOURSELF WITH SIMPLICITY AND CONSISTENCY — 45
- RUBY'S STORY — 47

CLEOPATRA — 51

- ADAPT BY LEVERAGING YOUR UNIQUE STRENGTHS — 57
- USE STORYTELLING TO WIN PEOPLE OVER — 59
- BE BOLD, BUT ALWAYS HAVE A STRATEGY — 61
- DIANA'S STORY — 63

ERNEST SHACKLETON — 69

- CRAFT BUOYANT MOMENTS OF CONNECTION — 76

REWRITE THE BLUEPRINT WHEN NECESSARY	**79**
ELEVATE THROUGH EMPATHY-DRIVEN LEADERSHIP	**81**
JACOB'S STORY	**83**

SUN TZU — 87

KNOW YOUR TERRAIN	**93**
ADAPT LIKE WATER	**95**
CHOOSE YOUR BATTLES	**96**
BEN'S STORY	**98**

JOAN OF ARC — 103

YOUR CORE BELIEFS ARE YOUR ANCHOR	**111**
TRANSFORM DOUBT INTO MOMENTUM	**114**
BE VISIBLE IN YOUR COMMITMENTS	**116**
NATALIE'S STORY	**118**

ALEXANDER THE GREAT — 121

TAKE BOLD, FEARLESS, DIRECT ACTION TO SOLVE PROBLEMS	**126**
IDENTIFY YOUR "EMPIRE"	**128**
LEAD FROM THE FRONT	**131**
ERIC'S STORY	**132**

GENGHIS KAHN — 137

LOOK FOR MERIT, AND FOCUS ON LOYALTY AND UNITY	145
BE OPEN TO LEARNING FROM ALL SOURCES	147
LEVERAGE PSYCHOLOGICAL ADVANTAGE IN NEGOTIATIONS	148
ELIZABETH'S STORY	149

EMPRESS WU ZETIAN — 153

TURN ADVERSITY INTO A STEPPING STONE	161
CHAMPION MERIT IN YOUR SPHERE	163
CHALLENGE NORMS WITH QUIET STRENGTH	165
AIDAN'S STORY	166

JULIUS CAESAR — 171

REDEFINE THE RULES WITH PURPOSE	176
MAKE YOUR WORDS STICK	179
CULTIVATE STRATEGIC PRESENCE IN EVERY ENCOUNTER	181
TERRY'S STORY	182

Introduction

"It is not the mountain we conquer, but ourselves."

- **Sir Edmund Hillary**

What is a "conqueror"?

The dictionary tells us that a conqueror vanquishes, defeats, or subjugates a people or a place, i.e., military conquest. But we can expand the definition and see that we conquer any time we **overcome or take control of something** – and that "something" could include our own weaknesses and fears. When we take our fate into our own hands, when we claim territory beyond our limits, and when we defeat those things that stand in the way of what we most yearn for, then we are conquerors.

Whether you have an ambitious professional goal, yearn to master an art or skill, or need the courage to overcome your own secret weakness or fear, **the classic military model of victory can reveal a lot about the nature of *psychological* victory**.

This book is all about the unique mindset and attitude most associated with overcoming adversity, triumphing in battle, and taking control, whether the battlefield is literal or allegorical. To this end, we will be examining the lives of ten key historical figures lauded for their ability to not only overcome obstacles but to rule over them.

Now, chances are that you don't have much in common with an ancient Mesopotamian king or an ancient Roman consul. And yet, each of us has a dragon to slay, a demon to overpower, or a mountain to climb. This is why our exploration won't stop at the legends of the great heroes of the past and will also include real-life, everyday examples of ordinary people living with bravery, self-definition, and purpose.

What does a conqueror do?

If you want to be physically fit, identify someone who is already fit, and do what they do. If you want to succeed academically or make a success of a new business venture, find people who have done just that, and emulate them. However, when it comes to true mastery, leadership, and self-determination, this approach is not enough.

Why? Because a conqueror never asks, "What do others do? What are the rules I should follow? Who is in charge and how shall I go about getting permission...?"

Rather, the great leaders and conquers of old were so successful precisely because *they did not do as others did*. They did not always follow the rules, nor respect prevailing authority. They defied conventions, reached for what they wanted, and pressed on, even when others were ready to give up in exhaustion or fear.

That is why this book will *not* contain a list of suggested tips and tricks you can try in order to mimic other people. Instead, we will be focusing on the *mindset* and *character* out of which certain actions predictably emerge. In cultivating that mindset in ourselves, we find our own authentic strength and conviction and become more like conquerors in our own right.

What does a conqueror do? Well, great men and women from the annuls of history have adopted widely differing strategies. *The Art of War* author Sun Tzu tells us to "ponder and deliberate before you make a move," but Julius Caesar might have countered with, "act first, ask questions later." Empress Wu Zetian of China might advise murdering your enemies; Catherine the Great would suggest inviting them to dinner, instead. Alexander the Great styled himself a divine son of Zeus, while Genghis Kahn framed himself as something akin to a natural disaster, claiming, "I am the punishment of god."

All these people conquered, but they did so in very, very different ways. What are we to make of these differences? That it's not the actions themselves, but the attitude that gives birth to those actions. Every life circumstance is different, and every challenge unique. Thus, a skilled and triumphant response will not always look the same.

Being a conqueror, then, is not a question of *what*, but of *how*. And that's what this book is all about.

How a conqueror thinks

In the chapters that follow, you will not find any lists, hacks, or step-by-step instructions. Instead, you will find something more valuable: questions.

This book cannot tell you what the most intelligent, most noble course of action is in your life right now. It cannot convince you to walk away from those things that are holding you prisoner, nor can it fight battles on your behalf. It can't magically remove what is currently frustrating or draining you.

What it *can* do, however, is prompt you to start seeking and claiming these things in yourself. *You* are the only person who can be a conqueror in your own life. In answering these questions, you begin the important inner work that with time will result in hard-won, genuine accomplishment. There is no cheat code. The historical greats mentioned in this book did not have one, either.

As with life itself, you get out what you put in. The greatest and truest ideas will only ever have value when *applied*, and applied skillfully. The conqueror doesn't just ask questions, but takes **inspired action** given the answers they discover. If you do nothing, this book will be an interesting, but forgettable abstract experience. If you ask yourself questions, if you seek to answer honestly and take action to apply what you learn, however, then you are already behaving like a conqueror–and you will be reading an entirely different book.

The details of what a conqueror does are largely unimportant–one course of action may be the right move in one context, and the wrong move in another. The conqueror mindset is what matters because it is what allows you to discern your best course of action in every moment, and seize that possibility with decisive and proactive control. A conqueror does not passively live out their lives inside pre-existing limitations. Instead, they redefine the limits. They forcefully reshape the narrative towards their own ends. *They make themselves.*

Despite their differences, the people in this book do have some notable traits in common. They've all possessed rock-solid self-belief and marched to the beat of their own drums. They were all, in their own ways, fearless, determined, and more than a little audacious. They made a name for themselves, and they did it with persistent, active strength. They all possessed the mindset of a conqueror.

By learning to think in the way they thought, we too can cultivate the rare attitudes, priorities, and perspectives that made them the successes they are. But first…

A caveat

Let's be blunt: Some of the people discussed in this book, though undeniable conquerors, are by no means always "good people." Ernest Shackleton's most famous voyage was a full-blown failure, and King Hammurabi sanctioned slavery. Alexander the Great had a drinking problem. Cleopatra killed three of her own siblings, Empress Wu killed her own baby, and Genghis Kahn killed… well, everyone.

Our list of ten notable conquerors includes wealthy aristocrats, murderers, and miscellaneous megalomaniacs. **We are not required to agree with or condone their lives in order to learn something from them.**

Not everyone on our list is even a "success" in their chosen field, nor are they a conqueror in every area of their lives. Many on our list racked up multiple failed marriages, had neglected social lives, and were horrible parents. We consider these people not because they might be moral role models, but rather because their lives serve as powerful archetypal representations of specific principles.

The people on our list demonstrate the power of certain perspectives, beliefs, and styles of living–those which, when applied more moderately, can bring success to our own lives. By observing the extreme lives of these historical figures, we can begin to distill those elements that set them apart and allowed them to conquer.

At the end of every chapter, you'll be encouraged to reflect and take inspired action in your own life. While these historical figures were certainly great in their own right, by the time you're done reading this book, I hope you'll have a strengthened sense of what your own "great" life looks like, and how you might conquer those things that are standing in your way. All that's needed is a little patience, an open mind, and the willingness to try something new. Let's dive in.

Catherine the Great

"One does not always do the best there is. One does the best one can."

- **Catherine the Great**

Ruling for 34 years, from 1762 until her death in 1796, Catherine, Empress of Russia, started life as a minor German royal. She would eventually overthrow her own husband, Tsar Peter III, to become one of the most celebrated and influential rulers in history. She was then, and is now, known as "the Great," but what exactly constituted her greatness? What made Catherine a conqueror?

To understand this, we need to understand a little about Russia at the time of her birth in May 1729. She was born Princess Sophie Auguste Friederike of Anhalt-Zerbst in Germany (more correctly, in the kingdom of Prussia), and was rechristened Catherine in 1744, when she converted to Russian Orthodox Christianity at 14. (We will stick with Catherine for our uses here.) Unlike other historical figures we'll explore in this book, she in no way came from humble beginnings. She was born into the ruling house of Anhalt, and her cousins Gustav III and Charles XIII reigned as kings of Sweden. Other members of her aristocratic family had also been installed as influential figures all throughout Europe.

However, although Catherine possessed this glittering lineage name, her family had little money, and her childhood was supported in large part by her mother's wealthy relations. While the princess was certainly born into privilege, she understood even as a child just how precarious that privilege really was. The European political elite that existed during the reign of the Holy Roman Empire consisted of a competitive and highly exclusive group of a mere 300 sovereign entities, who fought unceasingly to gain advantage over one another.

Within this group, political power and control was jealously guarded and reserved for the boys and men of the elect. This meant that a woman of noble birth typically had one means to obtain influence, security, or self-determination: marriage. Political or dynastic marriages of that era required all the strategy, cunning, intelligence, and bravery needed in literal battle–perhaps more. By carefully using her every advantage, Catherine was able to rule through the refined and delicate art of her class, that is, the **strategy of charm**.

Though reported to be a tomboy, Catherine would have been groomed from a very young age to one day become the wife of a powerful nobleman, and, in so doing, achieve some sort of advancement in the position of her family's name. She received a classical education and was tutored in multiple languages, as well as the most important skillset required of an 18th century princess: etiquette, decorum, and all the refined social attainments needed to navigate the complex social circuit of ballrooms and operas.

Her mother was a social-climber and gossip who had long schemed plots to install Catherine as the Empress of Russia. Catherine was just 10 years old when she met Peter III of Russia, who had been selected for her as future husband. She hated him. The marriage was part of a convoluted diplomatic intrigue to improve relations between Prussia and Russia, and to replace the chancellor Alexey Bestuzhev-Ryumin, thus weakening the Austrian alliance. The plan fell through in the end, but the marriage went ahead, and they were wed in 1745, when Catherine was just 16 years old.

The young girl arrived in Russia when she was 15 and immediately got to work ingratiating herself to all the right people. She learned

Russian, converted to Russian Orthodoxy, and was henceforth known as Grand Duchess Ekaterina Alekseyevna (Catherine Alekseyevna). She would later reveal in her memoirs that she was focused on undertaking whatever was necessary to attain the crown. Though Catherine alienated her own father by denying the faith she was raised in, her zealotry and dedication to her adoptive country's faith was soon common knowledge and won her a favorable reputation with the people. The young couple established themselves in the palace of Oranienbaum, and there they governed the small Schleswig-Holstein duchy in preparation to rule all of Russia.

Unfortunately, the marriage was a total flop. Catherine felt that Peter was immature and unattractive, and the union remained unconsummated for years. However, Catherine was reportedly not a romantic and did not truly desire her partners nor did she want a child–her real ambition was the crown. Though the couple eventually produced a legal heir, a son Paul in 1754, Catherine would go on to have numerous scandalous affairs and liaisons.

The couple largely ignored one another. Catherine took refuge in books, especially noteworthy philosophical works of the French enlightenment, such as Voltaire. Still a teenager, she read *Annals* by Tacitus and it laid the foundations for what would later become her own political philosophy, that is, an intelligent balance between pragmatism and idealism. Having been used as a political pawn herself since birth, Catherine had a deep and visceral appreciation for the idea that people never really act for the reasons they say they do, and to truly understand them, one needs to learn to read their hidden motivations.

Peter eventually succeeded to the throne in 1762 as Emperor Peter III, making Catherine the empress consort. However, the couple continuously worked against one another, both personally and politically, eventually living entirely apart. After six months of complicated political intrigue and conflict, Catherine orchestrated a coup wherein her husband was arrested and forced to sign a document of abdication of the throne. He was later assassinated in mysterious circumstances and, just eight days later, Catherine was crowned Queen. She would keep the throne until the end of her life, undefeated despite countless rivals and adversaries.

Catherine's power lay in her intelligence, wit, and ability to "play the game." She took Russia by force, from within the constraints that had been placed on her. She overthrew her own husband in a coup that required the skillful manipulation of numerous formidable powers and interests. Catherine was swift and constantly outmaneuvered her rivals, playing the field like a game of chess. In terms of sheer strategic prowess and tactics, it's hard to imagine a more adept mind than Catherine the Great's. She was a true conqueror, and **her genius was in fighting the battle she found herself in, with the tools she had.**

Catherine's life had never been easy, and she was plagued by opponents and deception. Usurpers were never far from her–her own son included–and intrigue followed her all her life. She suffered abuse at the hands of her mother, two miscarriages, and the death of an infant daughter when she was just 15 months old. Catherine died young herself and was her legacy was haunted by vicious rumors of her promiscuity and other unsubstantiated urban legends.

Nevertheless, as Empress, she would transform Russia entirely, ushering it into a new, enlightened era of art, science, and modernity. Her program to revolutionize Russia left its mark on the country, and she was loved by her people, who gave her the deferential title, "Mother."

Rule from the head

Catherine's intellect and pragmatism guided her rule. A self-taught student of the Enlightenment thinkers, Catherine forged a powerful combination of reason and practical governance. She introduced reforms that totally modernized

Russia, allowing it to spread its influence across the globe. Catherine was certainly ambitious and a studied idealist, but she knew precisely when to defer to practicalities: **She would never let her personal feelings of what *should be* interfere with her understanding of what *actually was*.** Catherine's reign was not a plot for personal aggrandizement nor an exercise in might; rather, Catherine ruled from the head, and her leadership heralded a new age in Russia.

Was Catherine just a scheming socialite? Was she merely a talented manipulator and dabbler in petty court intrigue? We can learn a lot by comparing Catherine with her mother, Joanna Elisabeth of Holstein-Gottorp, a woman who did indeed have a reputation for being meddlesome, and making rash decisions that ultimately jeopardized her social standing.

Though social and well-connected, Catherine's mother was known to be cold and even abusive. Catherine herself rose above all this, and was able to engage in political schemes without allowing emotion to distract her. "Study mankind," she said, "Learn to use men without surrendering to them. Have confidence in those who, if necessary, are courageous enough to contradict you."

Catherine didn't gossip and meddle; she networked. She mastered the arts of wit and charm, not to snatch little bits of other people's power, but to forge her own. Rather than getting embroiled in petty disputes and squabbles, Catherine learned to convert enemies into allies, all without upsetting the delicate political ecosystem on which her power depended. Literature professor and author Kelsey Rubin-Detlev says of the Empress,

> "[she] didn't just interact with public intellectuals: She was a public intellectual herself. She was a playwright, a journalist, a historian, a political theorist and much more. This is what being a great monarch in the Enlightenment was all about: combining ideas with power."

Showcase your bravery to inspire trust

Catherine was a student of the Enlightenment and ruled Russia in accordance with the principles of science, reason, and progress. So, when the smallpox epidemic threatened her empire, she became an advocate for the use of "variolation," which was an early form of inoculation against the disease.

Against prevailing fear and superstition, Catherine led the charge by personally taking the smallpox inoculation herself, proving both her commitment to her country and her trust in science. As the world had been ravaged by smallpox (and indeed, even Peter II had been disfigured by the disease), Catherine educated herself and had been inspired and influenced by

British doctor Thomas Dimsdale. Seeing how he had successfully inoculated the British Royal family, she desired the same for her own.

Her gesture was that of a brave scientist willing to stake her life on the principle of reason, and her attitude alone had a profound impact on Russian public health. By 1800, millions of Russian citizens had been inoculated, preventing untold suffering and death. Indeed, Catherine's advocacy earned her an additional title, "The Empress of Vaccinations."

If you're trying to rally your friends for something bold—say, organizing a beach clean-up or trying a new fitness challenge—go first. Dive into the cold water, carry the first bag of trash, or sign up for the class before anyone else. When people see your willingness to step up, they'll feel safer joining in, inspired by your example rather than just your words. And, when the project turns out to be a success, you will be remembered as its cause and trusted in the future to lead again.

- Considering your own life, in what ways might you be holding back, afraid to "make the first move"? Think about how you might broadcast your deeper values and principles not merely by talking, but by taking decisive action.
- A conqueror must first conquer themselves, especially when what is holding them back is

their own fear. That said, do your research, and seek the knowledge required to make a wise decision. Be honest about whether any hesitation in you comes from fear, a lack of understanding, or both.

- You don't have to make grand gestures and take big risks. You can inspire trust in small ways, too. If you can show, in small, everyday ways, that you are prepared to show up and go first, you demonstrate your willingness and ability to be a leader. Volunteer for things, reach out to someone first, or make suggestions. When you do, the rest of the interaction will be more on your terms than if you had waited for someone else to step in first.

Practice soft power

All of us will encounter adversaries, opponents, and naysayers, no matter how small or humble our intended project is. You don't have to be part of the treacherous political landscape of 18th century court life to encounter adversaries or people with interests that don't align with yours. Rather than getting upset about the existence of enemies (or even "frenemies") and wasting time and energy forcefully opposing them, take the smoother and easier approach of charming them.

From the start, Catherine understood the value of likability. She entertained and joked her way into the favor of even those assigned to spy on her; she hosted intimate dinners and playful gatherings to charm her allies and disarm her detractors. Whether hosting lively parties or penning witty love letters, she made herself approachable without losing her mystique as empress. Her ability to balance approachability with authority helped her forge alliances and gather invaluable intelligence.

It's possible to host successfully even if all you do is set up a potluck, game night, or book club. Invite friends, acquaintances, and that one person you've been meaning to connect with. Use the relaxed atmosphere to subtly steer conversations toward a shared goal, like planning a community event, organizing a group trip, or brainstorming a creative project.

Let the laughter and camaraderie do the heavy lifting for you—people will leave feeling connected and ready to align with your ideas. Instead of using force and coercion, maneuver people in such a way that they are unaware that they are being acted on at all. Help them to believe that the outcome that you most desired was actually their idea, or happened purely by chance.

To the conqueror's mind, the distinction between friend and enemy is a fluid one, and something discerned according to function and practicality. Don't avoid or mistreat people you don't like; instead, help them, and **make their success inseparable from yours**. In this way, you have created for yourself a grateful ally out of someone who might have otherwise opposed you.

Be strategic and deliberate in who you befriend, and find the advantage in even your worst critics and detractors. For some, such an attitude seems Machiavellian, but for Catherine, it was just a fact of life, and her relationships were no less valuable to her for being strategic.

Once, Catherine was being teased about "the blind obedience with which her will was fulfilled everywhere", but her response tells you everything you need to know about soft power:

> *"It is not as easy as you think. In the first place, my orders would not be carried out unless they were the kind of orders which could be carried out. I examine the circumstances, I take advice, I consult the enlightened part of the people, and in this way I find out what sort of effect my laws will have. And when I am already convinced in advance of good approval, then I issue my orders, and have the pleasure of observing what you call blind obedience."*

Catherine won over her spies by making them laugh and feel included. If someone in your circle is hesitant to support your idea—whether it's a book club, a volunteer project, or even a weekend hike—don't argue. Instead, invite them to something casual, like a trivia night or a coffee hangout, and focus on making them laugh. Slip in a comment about how much you'd love their input on your idea or how perfect they'd be for it. People are far more likely to join when they feel valued and entertained.

- Is there a social group, organization, or meeting that you really wish existed? Be courageous and set one up yourself.
- If you find yourself having to deal with someone difficult, think carefully. What are their goals? What do they value and how are they acting to achieve those things? Bringing them to your side may mean finding ways to *position yourself as a source of what they want, rather than an obstacle*. Instantly, you become allies.
- Smooth over awkwardness and uncomfortable moments with humor and lightness. Very often, conflict begins merely as a little friction, which you can easily shake off if you are calm, confident, and purposefully steering the tone of the interaction.
- Conduct yourself like an empress. Have impeccable manners, be gracious and polite, and do whatever you can to avoid vulgarity, gossip, or emotional outbursts. In the face of other people's rudeness, one of the most powerful things you can do is to maintain

your cool and respond with unexpected generosity and humor.

Find a balance

Some rulers fall because they are not leaders, but dreamers, mystics, or revolutionaries. They are inspired and stirred up by idealism, but their zealotry doesn't last. They burn out or are usurped by older, wiser conspirators. On the other hand, too much pragmatism also fails to create a leader. Too much realism and common-sense is dull and uncharismatic; what's more, a soulless bureaucrat may actually inspire mistrust, as people wonder about hidden motivations.

Catherine was *both* pragmatic and idealistic. She read voraciously and had lofty intellectual ideals towards which she pitched all her efforts. But, on the ground, she always knew when to concede to reality, when to compromise, when to wait, and when to make do with what she had, rather than wait for what might never come.

"You philosophers are lucky men," she told the French philosopher Diderot when he visited her in Russia. "You write on paper and paper is patient. Unfortunate Empress that I am, I write on the susceptible skins of living beings." She understood that the real world contained real people, with real time limits and other unyielding constraints. And so, if she wished to succeed, some concessions would be required.

Consider, for example, the complex situation of serfdom in Russia. Catherine was keenly aware of the injustices being done to the people, so she initially created policies and legislation to win their freedom. However, she soon realized that freeing the serfs completely would anger the noble landowners, and they were the ones she depended on to stay in power. If she offended them, she'd lose that power, and with it her ability to make a meaningful impact in the lives of the serfs. Thus, the only way forward would need to balance both interests.

Had she been a pure idealist, her sense of outraged injustice would have clouded her judgment and limited her impact. Had she been overly practical, she would have made herself a ruler indistinguishable from all the others, and easily replaced. So, she had to find a balance and tread the path somewhere between, keeping both serfs and landowners on her side.

- Don't be surprised by obstacles and setbacks; expect them and factor them into your plans. Remember that the grander the plan, the more formidable the obstacles. Preempt potential difficulty and work with it. For example, if you're launching a new project, proactively research any potential issues and plan a few steps ahead for how you will respond. You may even spot a way to turn those setbacks to your advantage.

- Are you stuck in the "planning phase"? To stop you from getting lost in abstractions and best-case scenarios, just jump in and take action, even if it's small. Instead of researching endlessly about a new career path, for example, just do the job. Offer your services for free, volunteer somewhere, or shadow someone else. Action will temper idealism.
- Think about a certain problem or stalemate you are facing in life right now. You may have decided that the issue is unresolvable, but is it? Look again at the problem with a little more pragmatism and ask, "If this is not working, then what *will* work?" Be curious and open-minded, and be willing to accept that certain plans, if they are to ever happen, may look quite different from what you'd ideally want.

Dan's story

Dan is a retired social worker who now heads a small charity that ensures that young kids have access to quality animated audiobooks online, for free. Though Dan had come far on his own ingenuity and resources, the time came to seek funding and sympathetic investors.

The trouble was, Dan hated having to make his case to such people. From his perspective, alleviating illiteracy and mitigating some of the effects of poverty on very young children was a cause that stood on its own merit, and he was more than a little frustrated that he had to "bring people round" to the cause he so passionately championed.

He'd get exasperated trying to navigate the complicated bid-writing process and would lose his temper with potential funders who seemed more interested in *appearing* charitable than actually being charitable.

One day, Dan was approached by an initiative that sought to put him in touch with a big-name academic at a university in the next town. The academic would apply for a research grant and employ some doctoral students who could then work for Dan. The university would win the fund, the academic would have something to publish, Dan would get the support and resources he needed... oh, and the children would ultimately get their free audiobooks.

Dan resented this plan, however, and felt deeply that he was being a "sell out." He quite rightly observed that everyone in this scheme was acting out of pure self-interest, and that in seeking a partnership with his charity, they were merely seeking to exploit his legitimacy. So when the research team invited him to an expensive dinner to discuss the matter, Dan turned them down.

Soon, a close friend pulled Dan aside and put it to him this way: The university *was* using him, but so what? Wasn't it also to his benefit? If the university bid was successful, then Dan would benefit… and that meant that the children would benefit, and isn't that what it was all about?

Dan accepted the invitation, and, keeping the children in mind, did his best to charm, entertain, and win over the research team, who at once got to work applying for funding in a far more effective way than Dan could ever have achieved on his own. The project was a success. Dan had initially assumed that being a conqueror in this situation meant fighting against the "system" and maintaining his ideological purity. Instead, he learned that sometimes, victory is not always black and white, but rather a compromise somewhere in the grey area.

Catherine the Great's conqueror mindset: "I play the game, but I never let the game play me."

Conqueror traits: Wit, charm, strategic diplomacy, balanced "soft power."

- Rule from the head, and do what you can with the cards you're dealt.
- Heroism and valor sometimes lie in the messy middle ground; find the balance between idealism and pragmatism.
- Be gracious, flatter, and use humor and generosity to take control.

Questions for reflection:

In what way can I "go first"?

How can I make my enemy's success inseparable from my own?

What do I need more of right now–pragmatism or idealism?

King Hammurabi

> **"The first duty of government is to protect the powerless from the powerful."**
>
> - **Code of Hammurabi**

Born almost 4000 years ago, King Hammurabi is certainly the most ancient of the historical figures we'll consider in this book. King Hammurabi of Babylon is today best known for creating one of the world's first written codes of law, the Code of Hammurabi. With its 282 laws inscribed on stone, the code was a revolutionary attempt to establish order in a world fraught with unpredictability.

From construction to trade to civilized social conduct, the code introduced principles of accountability and fairness that resonate even in modern management and governance. In fact, so much of what we now consider obvious when it comes to natural law, fair governance, and justice, is really the result of Hammurabi's tireless efforts so many millennia ago. Modern law and justice today are a mere continuation of the profound revolution brought about by King Hammurabi.

So, who was Hammurabi, and was it really such a big deal to write down some laws? Today, it's easy to think of the maintenance of the rule of law as a purely bureaucratic necessity, but far from being a mere autocrat, Hammurabi saw himself as a "shepherd" of his people, striving to balance authority with justice. His ability to **manage risk, align interests, and communicate clear standards made him not just a ruler, but a visionary in creating systems that endure.**

To truly grasp the depth of Hammurabi's contribution and leadership, we need to understand a little more about the world he ruled. A mere 40 years ago was well into the 1980s–a period still within memory. Now imagine ten times that, 400 years ago, that is, around the 1600s. This was the era of the Mayflower, the Civil War and the great fire of London–events that are distant, but still comprehensible to our modern minds. Now, try to imagine ten times that again, i.e., *4000 years back.*

Hammurabi lived an *extremely* long time ago. At this point in the human story, we were just entering the beginning of the Bronze Age.

Hunter-gatherers are settling down to invent agriculture and, in some cultures, to build more lasting settlements and monuments. The earliest forms of now extinct languages are still widely spoken, ancient Egypt has only just begun to think about mummification, and the Sahara Desert is going through a lush, green phase.

Crucially, writing has been invented, and we are thus at the dawn of what is considered "recorded history." We are at the very edge and limit of what can be known to historians today, and before this point lies darkness and conjecture. Indeed, Hammurabi's contribution was closely tied up with this new dawn of order and literacy in the great saga that is called human evolution.

Hammurabi of Babylon, Mesopotamia, was established as king in 1792 BC and ruled for 43 years, in that time expanding his kingdom and conquering many surrounding city-states. He then set to work governing his nation, and to do this, he created a system. We can know very little about Hammurabi as a person, yet his fairness and commitment to justice rings out in his Code of Hammurabi, today considered one of the earliest written documents.

Hammurabi was not democratically elected and modern sensibilities would consider him something of a dictator; however, it's important to remember that Hammurabi existed at a time when humankind was still trying to determine exactly how to organize and rule larger and larger collections of people. Hammurabi's genius was to understand the secret ingredient to successfully governing a true nation state–justice.

In the deepest, darkest recesses of history, might was right. It's hard for modern people today to understand to exactly what extent raw barbarism was the default; petty chieftains and family heads ruled over fractious warring tribes, who murdered, plundered, and raped as they saw fit. The powerful organized themselves into ruling clans and families, and women, children, and slaves were fair game in the endless squabbles and skirmishes over land and title.

This was the world that Hammurabi had inherited, and the world he would try to set to order with his Code. Thus, the book of law frequently emphasizes its central premise: Law is to protect the weak against the strong, to maintain order, and to regulate interactions. Ancient humans used to live in small bands of no more than 200 people, and they resolved their disputes on a personal level. Ancient Babylon, however, was the first city to reach of a population of 200,000 people–and Hammurabi knew that a more formal system governing their interactions would be required if peace was to be attained.

Consider this piece of prologue of the Code:

"When Anu the Sublime, King of the Anunnaki, and Bel, the lord of Heaven and earth, who decreed the fate of the land assigned to Marduk, the over-ruling son of Ea, God of righteousness, dominion over earthly man, and made him great among the Igigi, they called Babylon by his illustrious name, made it great on earth, and founded an everlasting kingdom in it, whose foundations are laid so solidly as those of heaven and earth; then Anu and Bel called by name me, Hammurabi, the exalted prince, who feared God, **to bring about the rule of righteousness in the land, to destroy the wicked and the evil-doers; so that the strong should not harm the weak**, so that I should rule over the black-headed people like Shamash and enlighten the land, to further the well-being of mankind [...] When Marduk sent me to rule over men, to give the protection of right to the land, I did right and righteousness in [...] and brought about the well-being of the oppressed."

Here we can see that Hammurabi was not simply an administrator trying to bring order to public affairs. Rather, he saw himself as a divinely appointed *creator* of that very order, as someone given the sacred mission to bring about true justice and uphold moral order. If the strong were permitted to behave in any way that they liked, a true kingdom could never prevail, and humanity would remain in its barbaric, "black-headed" condition. Progress and enlightenment, then, was intimately tied up with mercy, fairness, and civic duty. The law, for Hammurabi, was a moral entity.

Today, it's hard to imagine what we could learn from someone like Hammurabi and the world he lived in. However, we would do well to remember Sir Arthur Conan Doyle's words: "This world of ours appears to be separated by a slight and precarious margin of safety from a most singular and unexpected danger." The veneer of civilization is thin. Despite our loftier, modern intellectual endeavors, the fact remains that human nature requires a *practical* code of conduct to govern everyday dealings, so that the worst possibilities are everywhere curtailed.

Hammurabi's code was written in the Akkadian alphabet on a stone slab more than 7 feet tall. At the top was engraved an image of Shamash, the Babylonian sun god, and what follows is a list of conditional statements ("If this, then that") outlining proto law for criminal, family, property, and commercial cases. Some examples include:

- If a man accuses another man and charges him with homicide, but cannot bring proof against him, his accuser shall be killed.

- If a man has a debt lodged against him, and the storm-god Adad devastates his field or a flood sweeps away the crops, or there is no grain grown in the field due to insufficient water—in that year he will not repay grain to his creditor; he shall suspend performance of his contract and he will not give interest payments for that year.
- If a man takes in adoption a young child at birth and then rears him, that child will not be reclaimed.
- If a builder constructs a house for a man but does not make it conform to specifications so that a wall then buckles, that builder shall make that wall sound using his silver.
- If a free citizen should blind the eye of another free citizen, they shall blind his eye (that is, "an eye for an eye").

The 282 laws offer provisions for cases of assault, fair rates for hiring workers, building codes, family and inheritance disputes, land titles, the treatment of slaves, marriage, how to manage fraud or commercial deception, terms for loans, false charges, and the regulation of doctors, to name a few.

So, what are we to take from all this? Granted, to modern ears some of these laws seem trivial and petty–the kind of thing required to keep toddlers from squabbling. However, consider that today our governments are ordered and ruled by codes of law not dissimilar–in fact, modern codes are larger and more detailed than Hammurabi's.

Because of Hammurabi's laws, houses were built more safely, families were not as vulnerable to breakdown and abuse, and the mistreatment of slaves was curtailed. Because of Hammurabi's laws, a citizen could have some expectation of justice, no matter his own personal wealth or status. Thus, Hammurabi was not merely a conqueror of neighboring nations, but a conqueror able to subdue and rule over his own people's waywardness. We can see the core of Hammurabi's leadership principles, and the two things that allowed him to defeat disorder and lawlessness: accountability, and the means to communicate in transparent, reciprocal, and honest ways. Let's take a closer look.

Accountability, trust, and discipline

Some people will naturally behave with consideration for others. Some people will spontaneously do the more difficult or unpleasant thing instead of the easier, more appealing thing. For many people, however, there needs to be a system in place to ensure the right action, to guarantee accountability, and to inspire trust.

Imagine that you are an ancient Babylonian surgeon. You know that if you are negligent in your work, your patients could die, and you could be subject to harsh fines or, very likely, the death penalty. Granted, many doctors will automatically take care with their patient's lives, but the incentive of law ensures that those who don't still act with a minimum of responsibility.

We are often only able to do the right thing when we are truly incentivized to do so, i.e., we have skin in the game. Being accountable makes us disciplined, ordered, and willing to submit to an external standard. Today, the world is full of examples of corporations who bear no true accountability for their actions, and therefore they run rampant, grinding public trust down to zero. In Hammurabi's day, the builder of a poor house would himself be punished with his life; today, endless bureaucratic complexity means that nobody is truly accountable for anything, and when negligence or greed results in the death of thousands of people, it often appears that nobody at all is held responsible.

Hammurabi understood that accountability, incentives, discipline, and trust are all connected. Imagine, for example, the 2008 financial collapse. Millions of innocent people lost their jobs or their homes, and millions more were plunged into poverty. The financial institutions responsible, however, were not brought to justice. Today, these institutions are even less scrupulous than before, and public trust in them is even more desperately eroded.

This may be why author and economist Nassim Taleb mentioned the Hammurabi Code in a New

York Times piece ("End Bonuses for Bankers" November 7, 2011) on the crisis, saying,

> "...it's time for a fundamental reform: Any person who works for a company that, regardless of its current financial health, would require a taxpayer-financed bailout if it failed should not get a bonus, ever. In fact, all pay at systemically important financial institutions—big banks, but also some insurance companies and even huge hedge funds—should be strictly regulated."

It is a sentiment Hammurabi himself would condone. The bankers, in other words, need to have skin in the game. Wealthy bankers are able to take certain astronomical risks because they know that they will be rewarded no matter what; how differently they would act if the financial equivalent of "an eye for an eye" were applied to them!

Hammurabi's code is a way to govern a nation, but it has another, hidden power: **it can teach us how to govern ourselves.**

Hold yourself to high standards

Construction workers in Hammurabi's Babylon faced life-or-death consequences for shoddy work. Thus, houses were built to last. The power lies in the immutability of the standard; commit to taking responsibility for your own outcomes, even if there isn't someone literally waiting to dispense the death sentence if you don't follow through.

Hammurabi set the laws, but his end game was to have a nation of people who largely did not require them. In the same way, our lives can show this progression: We start with external laws, but the intention is to internalize them, and to eventually act righteously because it's become second nature to us.

If you're prone to procrastination, one way to think of cultivating discipline in yourself is to literally imagine that you're ruling over yourself much like Hammurabi ruled over his rebellious kingdom. At first, it might not work to appeal to your higher ideals or to hope that sheer willpower alone will be enough to get you to do the right thing. **Instead, use a little old-school law and order to *make* yourself do the right thing. In time, the right thing becomes habit. But until it does, rule yourself with an iron fist.**

- Hold yourself accountable in real ways and put some skin in the game. Don't allow yourself to get off scot-free like the 2008 bankers did. Instead, incentivize yourself so that your performance almost becomes a matter of life-and-death, just as it was with the Babylonian construction workers. It may sound like an extreme example, but try setting up a weekly direct debit to charity–a huge and uncomfortable sum. Then, arrange

it so that you have to report to a trusted accountability partner after every successful gym visit. Only they can pause the direct debit for that week. Over time, you will teach yourself exactly how accountability, discipline, and trust go hand in hand. Over time, you will internalize the habit.
- Devise your own personal code of conduct. The details don't matter too much; what's important is that you have rule of law that governs your behavior *no matter what*. These principles and life rules can apply to your personal life, or your business/work ethic. For example, "I never make a promise I cannot keep," or "I do not build software that I myself wouldn't use." Either way, writing these things down in black and white will not only give you more clarity and confidence in your own ambitions, but it will send a strong message to others about who you are, and what they can expect of you.
- Get rid of excuses. It's not popular in the modern world, but embrace the concept of shame, putting pride and honor in your ability to aspire to something better than the bare minimum. Be ruthlessly honest with yourself about whether or not your excuses are really just a cleverly veiled attempt to extract from a situation more than you intend to give. Consciously choose to build your identity on what you can and will do, rather than on what you cannot.

Organize yourself with simplicity and consistency

Compared to modern-day law, Hammurabi's codes were astonishingly simple and clear. They were intended to be jargon-free and accessible enough for the layman to comprehend. That said, there was seldom wiggle room; what was written was done.

You can take a page from Hammurabi's book–almost literally–by reminding yourself that the standards and rules we govern our lives with do not need to be sophisticated or complex. In fact, what matters most is that they leave no room for interpretation and can be followed consistently.

You can rule over your own world and conquer your own laziness or fear by simplifying your strategies. Write down your priorities in clear terms—no vague aspirations. Instead of "get healthier," commit to "walk 10,000 steps daily." Clarity turns overwhelming ambitions into actionable steps, building trust in yourself and your plans.

What's more, it cuts down the possibility of procrastination right at the root. Consider for example, that many goals and ambitions fail precisely because on an unconscious level, we never truly intended to achieve them. If we're hesitant about making commitments to ourselves, then we should be honest about *why*. Are we merely doing things we believe we "should"? Are we unprepared? Incapable? Plain old lazy?

Often, we make grand plans for ourselves and set ambitions and goals that *feel* good, but deep down we have not really committed ourselves. In this case, a humble, simple rule that we actually follow through on is far more powerful than a grand design that never amounts to anything.

- Rather than getting lost in soaring ambitions about the ideal life, ground yourself in the here and now, and the discipline required to navigate the everyday. Hammurabi knew that a well-functioning society needed organization on the bricks and mortar level. Set aside big visions and first just master the details of your daily routine: your bedtime, your meals, your commute. In what way can you cut down on "lawlessness" and a lack of order in your own life?
- Get detailed and get organized. Set up a proper budgeting system, and keep track of spending. Be diligent and detail oriented. Put numbers on things–calories, dollars, hours, whatever. What matters is that you are *governing* yourself in these matters, rather than letting chaos reign.
- Never be overwhelmed by disorder. Many conquerors must first conquer their own impulse to panic or throw in the towel when faced with something messy or chaotic.

Rather than despair at a lack of coherence or organization, consider it your God-given duty to find order, like Hammurabi. Take a deep breath, imagine a crown on your head, and *reign* over the situation. We are always sovereign when we can step outside the chaos and ask ourselves, "What do I want to happen here? What is the first step I can take to bring that about?"

Ruby's story

Ruby can scarcely remember her early twenties. With a background of trauma and abuse, Ruby's only survival mechanism had been to disappear into a blur of alcohol and drug addiction. One day she was talking to her long-suffering therapist who asked her bluntly, "And what is *your* responsibility in all this?"

Though the question stung, Ruby knew her therapist was right. What followed was a long road of yet more difficult questions. Ruby slowly discovered an unflattering truth about herself: She had been waiting all her life for someone to come and save her. In a deeply unconscious way, she had been expecting others to supply her with the kind of life she felt entitled to, and had gotten trapped in resentment about the various injustices of her childhood.

Ruby eventually realized that if she hoped to ever claw her way out of the mess of her life, she would need to be the one to do it. Through many long, hard months, Ruby challenged herself to take control of her own destiny. There was no longer any point railing against her past abusers or making excuses for her addiction problems.

She set to work building her life up from scratch, one day at a time. Though there were few role models in her world, Ruby decided that *she* would be that person for herself. She earnedlearned to cook healthy meals for herself. She took vitamins. She set up reminders. She signed up for regular AA meetings–daily ones, initially. She set up a network of friends to report to. She got a dog and whenever she felt like giving up, she reminded herself that this dog depended on her, and that it was up to her to wake up on time, and go for a walk, every single day, *no matter what.*

Over time, these little things gave Ruby a sense of real mastery, of dominion over herself. Yes, she would always be an addict, but she also knew that there were parts of her that were just, kind, and peaceful, and for the rest of her life, she would wake up and choose to put *those* parts of herself in charge.

Hammurabi's conqueror mindset: "Chaos is man's default. But I can live according to a higher law."

Conqueror traits: High and consistent standards, a sense of fair play, justice, transparency, practical accountability.

- Conquer yourself and have discipline; do not allow the lawless parts of yourself to rule over the better parts.
- Pay attention to the nitty-gritty and optimize your everyday routine.
- Hold yourself accountable to a higher standard.
- Maintain a sense of sovereignty and control amid chaos and disorder–be the first one to take responsibility.

Questions for reflection:

What system can I set up today to bring more order and discipline into my life?

In what practical ways do I need to get more organized?

Being completely honest, do I have "skin in the game"?

Cleopatra

"I will not be triumphed over."

- **Cleopatra**

Shakespeare painted Cleopatra's picture as an epic tragedy–one focused around the lovers in the titular *Antony and Cleopatra*. Old Hollywood tells us that she looked like Elizabeth Taylor, and that hers was a story of seduction and breathtaking splendor. We all "know" that Cleopatra bathed in milk and died by snakebite. And, in pop culture, she is cast variously as a villain, a figure of female empowerment, or a foxy Halloween costume option.

Historians, writers, and painters have always adored Cleopatra as a subject, but often superficially. Even today, the most pressing question people often have about this glittering figure is usually, "What did she look like? Was she beautiful? *How* beautiful?" The truth is that

Cleopatra was something far, far more interesting than all these depictions. Her real legacy lies neither in pomp and grandeur, nor in physical charm, but in her brilliance as a strategist, linguist, and ruler.

A descendant of the Ptolemaic dynasty, Cleopatra inherited a fractured kingdom and maneuvered her way to power despite familial treachery and external threats. With great effort and ingenuity, she maintained Egypt's independence amidst Rome's growing dominance.

Through shrewd alliances, most notably with Mark Antony and Julius Caesar (who we will discuss later in this book), Cleopatra pushed Egypt to the very brink of becoming a colossal force in the Mediterranean. During her reign Egypt had become a superpower, with prosperity and progress in the arts, mathematics, philosophy, and science. Egypt housed new translations of world-defining texts from all across the globe. Cleopatra's–and Egypt's–downfall came at the hands of Rome's inevitable expansion, but her legacy endures as a symbol of intelligence, adaptability, and resilience.

Cleopatra's full name was Cleopatra VII Thea Philopater, which translates literally from the Greek as "father-loving goddess." She was born around 70 BC and ruled Egypt for 21 years until her death at the young age of 39. Cleopatra was a descendent of Ptolemy I Soter, a Greek general who served in the companion calvary of Alexander the Great.

Cleopatra was born in Alexandria in the Ptolemaic Kingdom, and she was the last pharaoh to rule during the Hellenistic period, which came to a close with her death in 30 BC. Just one year after Cleopatra's death, the Battle of Actium saw the Romans destroy the last remnants of the Ptolemaic kingdom, demoting Egypt to a province of the Roman Empire. She was survived by her four children, her firstborn the famous Caesarion, son of Julius Caesar, and a legacy so captivating that it's still the stuff of legend today.

Through all this, it's hard to imagine that Cleopatra was a mere mortal. Who *was* she?

What was her personality like, and what was it that allowed her to live the life she led?

Consider the kingdom that Cleopatra inherited along with her illustrious titles. Today, people are dazzled by the majesty, splendor, and beauty of ancient Egypt, but the truth is that Cleopatra's world was vicious, violent, and full of treachery.

In the dynastic elite in which Cleopatra was born, murder and treachery was the norm, and ancient Egyptian history is replete with tales of mothers going to war with their own children, brothers and sisters murdering one another, and legitimate heirs squabbling amongst themselves and plotting one another's assassinations. Cleopatra's great-grandmother launched a bloody civil war against her own parents, and later launched another against her own children. Cleopatra would eventually follow suit and have her co-ruling brother and royal consort murdered, along with a sister who herself had murderous plans to steal the throne. Cleopatra's own family was a pit of vipers, and she had no allies in a complex world of rapidly shifting allegiances.

The odds were against her from the beginning. She constantly strove to outmaneuver usurpers and adversaries, and find a way to preserve her family line. She was a woman in a man's world and what's more, her job was to maintain Egypt's peace and independence as a tenuous "client kingdom" of the most powerful empire in the world at the time–Rome. It's no exaggeration to say that everything was out to get Cleopatra.

And yet, she prevailed.

At the time of Cleopatra's reign, it was common to cast oneself as a divinity, and it's almost possible to imagine that there really was something otherworldly about Cleopatra. Stacy Schiff, biographer and author of *Cleopatra: A Life*, believes that **Cleopatra's tale is ultimately about the heroism of survival**. What Cleopatra so elegantly teaches us is that the brain is the most powerful survival organ, and the Egyptian queen was a genius at navigating almost unthinkable amounts of stress and danger.

In 48 BC, Cleopatra's brother was sitting on the throne, after having banished her to a desert in what is now Syria. She was only 21 years old, both her parents were dead, and she had had to run for her life into exile. Camping in tents, Cleopatra was resourceful enough to raise a band of mercenaries for an army and defeat her brother in a naval battle. Astonishingly, she then forced her sister into exile, potentially murdering her. For a time, Cleopatra ruled with the youngest and her only remaining brother... until he mysteriously died from poisoning. Cleopatra would later share the throne again, with her young son Caesarion, but by that point there was no question that she alone was the real sovereign.

Cleopatra's mastery of adaptation and languages was her greatest strength

Faced with the constant threat of extermination, Cleopatra's ability to pivot and recalibrate ensured her survival in a volatile world. In her day, Greek was the language of bureaucracy and business, and so fluency was required of the Egyptians. Ruling elites would typically not speak Egyptian, but seeing that the 7 million people she ruled over spoke it as their mother tongue, Cleopatra devoted herself to studying it, not unlike Catherine the Great did with Russian.

She was the only one of her line to ever do such a thing. In fact, Cleopatra was a polyglot and fluently spoke *eight* languages, which undoubtedly allowed her to open countless doors and build trust with foreign powers. Her charm and eloquence captivated allies, including both Julius Caesar and Mark Antony, enabling her to forge relationships that ultimately fortified her reign.

Cleopatra controlled the narrative

Her proficiency with languages was strategic. Because Cleopatra worked so hard to understand Egyptian culture, she was able to completely align herself with the image of the Goddess Isis, anointing herself as a divine source of wisdom, life, and material sustenance.

Cleopatra was confident, prepared, and shrewd, and she understood above all the power of *image*. Cleopatra had style. But this was no simple vanity or luxury; rather, Cleopatra was masterful at framing and manipulating the narrative she would need in order to maintain power and adapt as necessary. She knew how to make an entrance, to capture and keep attention, to hold court, and to use vast, expensive displays of grandeur to elevate herself to the status of a sensation.

Cleopatra framed her narratives with precision, aligning herself with the Egyptian aesthetic to inspire loyalty and trust among her people. Her talent for framing and persuasion made her a force to be reckoned with in both domestic and international politics. Cleopatra did not do things timidly or by half measure, and she was not afraid to be visible–extremely and demandingly visible.

Adapt by leveraging your unique strengths

Is everyone capable of being a Cleopatra? Of course not. The world she lived in is now lost to antiquity, and there will never be another Cleopatra. But this, in fact, is the point: Cleopatra was herself, and nobody else. We achieve something of her power when we grasp our own uniqueness in this way.

When it comes to finding your way through a cut-throat environment, there is sometimes no other strategy but to seek out and amplify those very skills and attributes that none of your competitors will possess. Cleopatra took her ability with languages and converted it into deep insight into the character and soul of her nation. With that insight she modelled herself into an ostentatious vision of the reincarnated Goddess Isis herself. She gave herself the regal title *New Isis* and donned evocative regalia to leverage the deeply embedded theology of the time that saw royalty and divinity as tightly interconnected. Cleopatra was able to control this narrative because she was able to *understand* it first.

We do not live in ancient Ptolemaic Egypt, but we nevertheless live in a world dominated by narratives. We can take a page from Cleopatra's book by carefully considering the most potent narratives around which the world around is organized and seeking to align ourselves in ways that cement and secure our own power.

This is not as deceitful as it sounds; consider that Cleopatra most likely sincerely believed that she *was* the reincarnated Goddess, and took her role as spiritual custodian of Egypt extremely seriously. But still, she left nothing to chance, and was deliberate in her role and persona, understanding exactly how to position and frame herself for maximum impact.

- Identify a skill or trait that truly sets you apart, for example in your workplace. What is something that you can do (or are simply willing to do) that others can't or won't? This is a way to completely distinguish yourself. Don't be afraid to be set apart–often, we unconsciously hide or downplay all the things that make us different, when these things are really our greatest assets.
- You can become masterful at "languages" without necessarily learning a whole new tongue. Carefully think about new ways to communicate effectively with those around you, especially those that you want to impress and keep on your side. Carefully consider people's values, perspectives,

needs, and intentions, and then speak to their perspective. Can you learn a little more about their in-jokes, slang, and expressions?
- Don't be afraid to blow your own horn, so to speak. Cleopatra led with the kind of confidence that only comes from believing that you are, quite literally, a goddess walking among mere mortals. While arrogance and overconfidence can be dangerous, there is something powerfully magnetic about self-belief this strong. Hold your head high.

Use storytelling to win people over

The stories of Cleopatra's life are compelling and have been told and retold. Stories are everything; they inspire hope, trust, loyalty– even fear. Cleopatra didn't set herself apart from the Egyptian worldview and belief system, but rather seized it and made it her own, crafting a mythology in which she claimed the starring role.

Leaders who possess a true conqueror mindset understand that a good story is far, far more effective at changing hearts and minds than an army of thousands. Consider the story of Cleopatra arranging to meet Caesar by being smuggling away inside a rolled-up carpet. Not only did the vivacious 21-year-old Cleopatra instantly charm the unsuspecting Caesar, but she also simultaneously set in motion a story of elevated love and intrigue that is still a perennial theme for songs and paintings.

Or consider her extravagant entrance into Rome, a mind-boggling scene now immortalized in the 1963 movie *Cleopatra*. While the film depiction is not entirely accurate, what resonates is the story that Cleopatra was telling by such an audacious arrival into Rome, and what her gesture signified politically.

The queen and her young son, clad in gold and bedecked in evocative religious regalia, arrive in outstanding pomp and ceremony, before bowing to the emperor Mark Antony. The emperor, who considered himself the embodiment of Dionysus, beheld a woman who had styled herself as the goddess Aphrodite. The story is told without uttering a word: "Rejoice because here I am, your equal and counterpart. I submit, but from my own glorious sovereignty."

- In your life, deliberately create compelling stories that showcase your goals and values in the most advantageous light. If you're pitching an idea, don't just present data—tell a story about how your vision could transform the team's success. Stories stick; facts alone often don't.
- Though it may feel a little unnatural, devise a coherent story about your own life and purpose that bypasses the ordinary and speaks directly to the emotions. Is yours a

tale of overcoming? One of strength or grace? Of daring? Always remember that *you* get to tell that story. Rechristen failures as learning moments, or flaws as endearing quirks that make you the individual you are. The details sometimes don't matter all that much if at the end of the day they constitute a good story!

- Consider also the stories that *other* people live by. If you are dealing with a rather egotistical boss, for instance, you might notice that they consider themselves a great leader and teacher. To best connect with them you understand that you need to tap into this story; you frame your requests in terms of "asking for help," knowing that this is the only way they will be received.

Be bold, but always have a strategy

Cleopatra's dazzling barge entrance to meet Mark Antony wasn't just about luxury—it was a calculated move to leave an unforgettable impression. To follow in her footsteps, try to bring a little strategic boldness into your own life. It's worth stating here that boldness is *not* the same as arrogance, carelessness, or delusion. Boldness is not about flinging yourself into danger with haughtiness and pride.

Rather, boldness as a strategy is about *calculated* risk-taking and exposure. **When you are bold, you communicate with others a powerful message of your own conviction and**

confidence. You demonstrate vigor and willingness to act. This has a strange effect on people, and they start to really believe that you "have something."

In Cleopatra's world, there was no room for timidity, second-guessing, or hesitation. Consider, after all, the sheer nerve you would need to murder your own brother and sister, to single-handedly lead an army, or to call yourself a goddess. Even a little of Cleopatra's chutzpah could go far in our own lives!

When you are bold, you demonstrate faith in your own purpose, and confidence in your own entitlement to that purpose's fulfilment. It is a posture natural to a conqueror because it speaks to deep, internally derived strength and validation. Rather than waiting for others to give you permission to shine, you take the first step and put yourself out there with pluck and daring.

Rather than wasting time thinking about fashions and conventions, worrying about creating offense, or hanging back out of fear that you may regret it, be bold. Remind yourself of your purpose, and act. You are not a pharaoh of Egypt, but you are sovereign ruler of your own life, so claim that power and take decisive–informed–action.

- Think of ways you can make a bold statement, but with purpose. Could you be the one to speak out loud what everyone else is afraid to admit? Could you take the risk of reaching out to someone first, and laying all your cards on the table? Could you stand up and boldly claim a role for yourself, share a plan, or offer an insight? Could you ask for more money than you originally planned?

- If you're interviewing for a job, don't settle for generic answers; present a clear, standout idea that shows you've thought deeply about the role. You don't have to be controversial, but don't be afraid to provoke a little heat. Boldness combined with intent, like Cleopatra's, can shift the balance of power in your favor. Make people sit up and pay attention.
- Originality means being bold enough to go beyond conventions and expectations. Being bold doesn't always have to be flashy and dramatic. In fact, sometimes it can be incredibly quiet and still. If you're feeling peer pressured into something, you can show your boldness by quietly resisting what goes against your values. Stand up for yourself, state an unpopular opinion, and be brave enough to sometimes do what is unexpected.

Diana's story

The day that Diana received the call that she'd nailed her interview and she was being offered her new job, she couldn't quite believe it. She was in her early twenties, fresh out of college and had barely any experience. She would be joining a team of professionals who had won awards, published books, made names for themselves, and regularly appeared in the media. She was thrilled… and more than a little intimidated.

In preparation to start work, she brushed up on her skills, bought a new work wardrobe and looked forward to learning from the best in the industry. But this was not at all what happened. Instead, Diana would forever remember her first day as a nasty shock; her workplace had none of the glamor and prestige it conveyed outwardly. Instead, she found that she was met with hostility and indifference.

Diana was an immigrant and had a noticeable accent. She was one of just three women on a team of more than fifty, and before the first week was over, she had become painfully aware of hurtful rumors, snide comments and "helpful suggestions" about her clothing choice, her manner of speaking and the quality of her work. People shamelessly plagiarized her work or stole it outright, and, astonishingly, she started to wonder if a certain senior staff member was actually aiming to get her fired–a woman, no less.

By the time she received her first paycheck, she was distraught and seriously wondering whether she should call it quits. She had studied diligently for years and had yearned for this role, yet now everything seemed tainted. But, like Cleopatra, Diana's sheer stubbornness allowed her to forcefully affirm to herself, "I will not be triumphed over."

It took some time, courage, and plenty of sleepless nights, but Diana soon realized that if she wanted this dream job, she would have to fight for it. She became curious about the bullies and bigwigs in the office, and studied them closely. She would not get angry, and she would not be afraid. Instead, she began to closely examine her colleagues as combatants. Rather than passively react to the injustices they were flinging her way, she would be proactive and make her own strategy.

Over the course of the year, Diana slowly but surely changed the narrative. When people commented about her age and made insinuations about her lack of experience, she would *thank* them for acknowledging her youth and agree that a fresh approach was just what the company needed. When it was implied that she was less capable of her job because she was a woman, she went out of her way to quietly resolve stubborn issues in a manner that only a woman could. She identified the most influential team members and endeared herself to them, deliberately tweaking the way she framed her appeals to suit her audience.

After a year of office drama and intrigue, Diana was growing weary, but mere survival had never been her only goal. She had a plan. Within 2 years she left her job with glowing references from key individuals in the organization. Having closely observed serious flaws in the industry from the inside, she quickly established herself as an independent consultant and deliberately targeted female clients who had felt intimidated and belittled when working with her former colleagues.

What's more, Diana had taken the time to carefully create a brand image that was utterly unique; she styled herself as a brave entrepreneur who had beaten the odds in a male-dominated world, and now she was going to revolutionize the entire field by offering expanded, custom-made women-only services that nobody else in the business was offering.

Soon, it was Diana who was speaking in interviews and being asked to submit articles, and people connected with her tale of gender discrimination in a cutthroat industry. Diana was certainly hardworking and intelligent, but it was her *story* that spoke to people. Her corporate experience had been difficult and unpleasant, but she had chosen to rechristen that struggle as a trial-by-fire that ultimately left her stronger. Diana had begun her career as a victim, but she refused that narrative. She would not have others thrust that role on her. Instead, she would be a conqueror.

Diana had committed to good storytelling, to controlling the narrative, and to refusing to be dominated. All this was neatly encapsulated in the logo she chose for her consultancy: a half-moon with bow and arrow. These are both symbols of the mythical Diana, the archetypal huntress and evocative figure of feminine capability.

Cleopatra's conqueror mindset: "I am in charge. I decide how the story ends."

Conqueror traits: Self-preservation and survival, healthy self-belief, boldness, verbal and symbolic literacy.

- Identify your unique strengths and boldly broadcast them.
- Figure out how to "speak people's languages" and tap into myth and storytelling to capture attention.
- Pay attention to image and present yourself accordingly.

Questions for reflection:

What narrative can I tell to showcase my most unique talents?

How can I reframe my current failure or setback in a completely different way?

In what ways can I be more strategically and boldly visible as the person I am?

Ernest Shackleton

"Men are not made from easy victories but based on great defeats"

- **Ernest Shackleton**

More than a hundred years ago, a young Ernest Shackleton embarked on a voyage to Antarctica. It was 1914, and the Anglo-Irish explorer found himself in the middle of what is now called the Heroic Age of Antarctic Exploration–and indeed, Shackleton would one day be called a hero. But the mission for which he would be remembered was actually a complete failure. Despite unthinkable peril and danger, Shackleton took charge and led all 27 men safely home again, even though the mission itself went wrong in every conceivable way.

Today, Shackleton is probably the most well-known explorer of old, and has become an almost legendary figure of superhuman leadership in extreme circumstances. Shackleton's story is a poignant reminder: **We distinguish ourselves and forge our character as conquerors not by avoiding failure, but in the way we *respond* to failure.**

Shackleton did not demonstrate any virtuosic abilities as a child, nor did his upbringing reveal any clues that he might one day become a man of renown. In fact, the opposite was true. He was born in County Kildare in Ireland in 1874 as the second of ten children. He read voraciously and showed an early interest in adventure stories, but was not an accomplished scholar, and was restless and bored with his schoolwork. He was eventually permitted to leave school at 16 and seek his fortune on the sea. His father managed to arrange a berth with the Northwestern Shipping Company, aboard *Hoghton Tower*.

He spent the next four years at sea, learning his trade, meeting new people and eventually passing the exam to become ship's second mate. He moved through the ranks to third officer, then obtained his first mate's ticket, and finally qualified as a master mariner, which meant he could command a British ship anywhere in the world.

By the time he was 24 years old he was working a mail and passenger carrier line between Britain and South Africa. When the Boer War broke out in 1899 he transferred to troopship Tintagel Castle. In March 1900 he met the son of

Llewellyn W. Longstaff, who was the financial backer for the British National Antarctic Expedition. Shackleton was instantly drawn to the idea and managed to obtain an interview with Longstaff to beg for a place on the expedition.

His pluck and persistence paid off, and he was eventually accepted by Sir Clements Markham, the man mainly responsible for organizing the expedition. It was 1901 when his place was confirmed. His career as a Merchant Navy officer was concluded, and he began his new life as sub-lieutenant in the Royal Naval Reserve on the ship *Discovery*.

It was Shackleton's third Antarctic expedition, however, that proved the most fateful. It was now 1914, and the ship *Endurance* was set to sail for the South Pole via Argentina. The crew would walk across the continent, and meet another crew who would collect them on the other side. Shackleton certainly had experience and was prepared, and the crew would have had state-of-the-art equipment. However, it's worth remembering that these early explorers attempted their feats entirely without radios, snowmobiles, or other high-tech gadgets. Instead of the modern waterproof winter gear we might take for granted, these men wore reindeer fur, beaver skins, wool, and canvas. Food was sparse and tightly rationed, and quarters on board were cramped and freezing cold.

Nevertheless, they made it to Argentina and then set off again for a small whaling station on South Gorgia Island. Here they were informed by the whalers there that the Weddell Sea was currently jammed with more ice than had ever been recorded. The crew waited a month to see if conditions improved, but when they didn't, they decided to press on anyway.

Six weeks after setting out, they found themselves horribly stuck in the ice. The hard ice spanned for miles in every direction, and pinned them solidly in place, "like an almond in a bar of chocolate." Panic slowly set in. They were more than 1000 miles away from any help, and there was no way to signal their distress. They were completely, utterly alone in a hellish winter landscape that would not release them.

The crew did what they could to cut through the ice, but even their most valiant efforts only scratched the surface of the problem, and they could not break free. There was no choice: They would have to spend the winter aboard, and wait.

For ten long months they waited. As the days crept on, they waited for spring, and watched with growing terror as their supplies dwindled. Eventually, they resorted to hunting to survive; eating seals and penguins, limping along day after day, week after week. Though challenging, however, the crew was hopeful and resilient, with many crew members later sharing in biographies how these months had been some of the best of their lives.

But eventually, fate intervened and the situation took a turn for the worse. In October 1915, the ice that had trapped them began to shift dangerously, and threatened to crush and damage the ship. The writing was on the wall, and the crew hastily made their way out and onto the ice. The ship sank three weeks later.

All 28 crew members were now stranded on a floating ice floe in the middle of nowhere, with nothing but three small lifeboats, a little gear, and barely any provisions. By this point, the men knew that everyone back home would have assumed the voyage a failure and the crew dead; nobody was coming to save them. It's hard to imagine the crushing weight of this realization, but Shackleton had to face the truth; if they wanted to keep their lives, they would have to save themselves.

First, they made a few attempts to reach a nearby resupply station, but the ice was constantly shifting, cracking, and splitting, forcing them to abandon the plan. Instead, they crammed into the lifeboats and sailed north for Elephant Island. It took 16 death-defying days, and the crew arrived only to discover that there was nobody there who could help. The crew were not just physically exhausted and starving, they were rapidly running out of hope.

Shackleton eventually chose five other men and took the one lifeboat still in good working condition to traverse the 800 miles of Weddell Sea to reach the South Georgia Whaling station. This took a further three weeks, and throughout the ordeal the men battled demoralization and fear of what they would, or wouldn't find, on arrival. From that station, Shackleton thankfully succeeded in arranging a rescue ship, but this alone took a further four months. When he was finally able to return to Elephant Island, every one of the 22 crew members he had left there was still alive and waiting. It was an unimaginable relief.

The voyage had been an unmitigated disaster, and had tried the men's resilience to breaking point at every juncture. And yet, it was this voyage that made Shackleton the inspiration he still is today. Every man survived, and it was in no small part due to Shackleton's' masterful handling of the situation, no matter how dire it became.

Shackleton led with relentless optimism

Most people can maintain hope and endure hardships for a little while. However, it takes something special to remain optimistic after *continued* disappointments, setbacks, and challenges. Shackleton didn't merely survive a single disaster, but rather a long, long string of disasters that unfolded one after the other over the course of months.

As the men grew ill, weak, and tired, they also began to lose confidence in themselves and their mission. As their resources dwindled and they lost weight and strength, it was natural to let doubt creep in a little more each day. Shackleton, however, maintained an iron-grip on his unwavering belief that they *would* find a way out, and that they *would* prevail.

At times like these, logic is no comfort, and there is no satisfying argument you can make to boost morale–after all, all the "facts" pointed to a thoroughly hopeless situation. Instead, it was Shackleton's stubborn refusal to collapse into despair, and his unwavering courage that kept his crew going. He worked constantly to keep up good cheer with jokes, stories, and songs. He cherished the camaraderie between the men as though their lives depended on it–because it did.

Hope under pressure is, in many ways, irrational. But there is a genius that goes beyond this, and it is the genius of loyalty, strength, commitment, and faith. This is what made Shackleton a true conqueror, even as he did not technically succeed on his mission.

That said, hope was no abstract or feeble thing for Shackleton. On the contrary, his optimism and good cheer was a deliberate way to prioritize his team's wellbeing. **At some point, the mission changed.** The new plan was to *survive*, and that would require responding decisively to a whole new reality. Shackleton's ability to move on and adapt is poignantly illustrated in the sinking of the *Endurance*; many hopes and plans went down into the ocean along with that ship. And yet the men lived. Sometimes, life presents us with paradoxes like this, and we must choose to fail initially if we wish to ultimately succeed.

Craft buoyant moments of connection

Shackleton was proficient at his work and was intelligent and technically skilled. However, when push came to shove, it was his ability to lead his team that allowed him to conquer adversity. He was well liked and knew how to keep spirits high and lively. Shackleton spent night and day with his crew mates, he ate with them, he worked with them, and he shared triumphs and trials with them. Shrewd problem-solving would get them out of their dilemma, but they would never be able to function well as a team unless they first had loyalty and morale. And that's what Shackleton was able to nurture.

Shackleton was likeable and approachable. He wanted every member of his team to know that they could trust him, and come to him for anything. He made time to know them and understand them, and took great care to maintain strong cohesion, snuffing out any tension or stress that would threaten the mission.

Most of us are *untested*. We have not experienced a real emergency or crisis, and we have never had to dig deep to find courage in dire and unpredictable circumstances. But in life's truly decisive moments, it may be that **our ability to thrive when times are ideal is not as important as our ability to survive when they are not.**

Physical exhaustion is dangerous, but disillusionment, disappointment, and despair can undermine the efforts of a person who isn't even exhausted yet. Fear and uncertainty can threaten group cohesion and rapidly drain away a team's energy. But with the right leader, people can push on and do more than they ever thought possible.

To replicate some of this spirit in your own life, think carefully about how you cope under pressure, disappointment, or outright failure. Remind yourself that *the mission has changed*. If the ship is sinking, let it sink, but don't become immobilized by despair and regret about its loss. Quickly pivot to the next mission.

- Pay attention to the mood and morale of your team and group. Even small gestures can completely change the tone and vibe of a team. Use humor, be complimentary,

encourage community, and use your voice to draw attention to the positive.
- If the challenge you are facing right now is a faltering of your own courage and strength, then realize that it's in your power to give yourself the things you need to boost your spirits. This may not feel natural or comfortable at first, and that's why a little stubbornness is needed! Forget about the problem for a while and call up a friend for a night out or a favorite meal. Reach out to someone you've lost touch with and find a way to bond with them. Fill your spirits by listening to a feel-good song playlist, or watching funny videos or comedy. These moments of levity may seem irrelevant when you're facing a crisis, but they can deeply anchor relationships and reinvigorate purpose. Whatever dilemma you're facing, it will seem so much more conquerable after you've fed your spirit this way.
- If you're feeling gloomy and stuck, try shifting your perspective. You can "own" your adversity, and you can decide on the frame you want to bring to it. After all, many terrifying and truly dangerous situations are later recounted with glee and re-classified as high adventure, remembered forever as "the best times of my life." Realize that you have immense power to adopt whatever attitude you like towards adversity. You can decide to draw closer to others, to lift them up, to have

hope, to move with energy and purpose, and to be a force for good. You can do that whether the mission is going well... or failing spectacularly.

Rewrite the blueprint when necessary

When Shackleton's mission became untenable, he adapted. Often, the trouble is not people's inability to cope with disaster in a practical way, but the *psychological* inability to process that loss and move on from it swiftly. We may waste time arguing with our new reality, or get stuck in denial. We may feel blindsided, insulted, or embarrassed, but if we get distracted complaining about the injustice of it all, we miss out on real opportunities for growth.

In your life, **practice recalibration—if an ambitious plan flops, redefine its trajectory without hesitation**. Whether it's altering a fitness routine to suit a new schedule or rethinking how to resolve a family conflict, embracing fluidity often reveals new and unexpected pathways. It keeps us moving and one step ahead.

Granted, it's not always easy to cut your losses and make a dramatic shift, especially if you've invested in a particular outcome. But remind yourself that Shackleton's fame and success was *not* outcome dependent. It hardly mattered why they failed, or who was to blame, or what they could have achieved instead. The mission was a disaster, but what mattered was what they made of that failed mission *afterwards*. When Shackleton set sail, he had hoped and planned for a successful Antarctic mission. Instead, what he got was a hair-raising tale of triumph in the face of desperate danger–after months and months, the Antarctic mission was the furthest thing from the crew's mind.

Don't be afraid to shift the terms, change goals, or reset your frame of reference. There's no point thinking about what *could* have or *should* have been. Instead, apply yourself with curiosity to what *is*, and how you can make the very best of it.

- Take back control and be decisive about calling off something that simply isn't working anymore, even if it feels like a loss to change trajectories. If, for example, a business idea has stalled or flopped, or if you've had to swallow an enormous financial setback, be courageous and *accept it*. Forgive yourself, make peace with that loss, and you will conquer your own disappointment.
- Be honest if other people's expectations are keeping you limited or trapped in compromises that are no longer working for you. It's easy to chain ourselves to big ambitious plans and forget that there are always multiple routes to the things we value. In a roundabout way, Shackleton found fame and success as an explorer. Think

about the deepest values you're striving towards and ask if there are more ways to attain those things than you're currently admitting.
- Many of us have rather narrow ideas about what successful people look like. For example, we think that explorers must be fearless, rugged individuals. But not Shackleton: his was a social, relational genius, and his strength was his emotional intelligence. Thinking of your own life, in what ways can you challenge the conventional image of "success"? Might there be other ways to demonstrate your excellence?

Elevate through empathy-driven leadership

In an emergency, people can slip into fear-based decision making. In a panic, they can start to behave rashly and recklessly, unwittingly causing more harm than good. A CEO of a failing business, for example, might become so fearful and fixated on the bottom line that they start mistreating their employees. In their desperation to save money, they end up insulting and alienating the only people who can make that money in the first place.

Empathy-driven leadership, on the other hand, is more holistic than this. It's not merely a question of prioritizing people over practicalities–it's the realization that you take care of practicalities by taking care of people.

When he nurtured the wellbeing and morale of his team, each and every one of them was able to pull through out of starvation, illness, and deep fatigue.

Too often, our models of leadership are based on flimsy ideas about what leadership actually is. Perhaps we imagine a mighty ruler perched on a throne high above his underlings. Maybe we think that leadership is something more like *control* or *management* of people in the way you would see the functioning of cogs in a machine.

Shackleton possessed empathy and sensitivity to his men, however, and was attentive to their emotional needs, their weaknesses, and their fears. In other words, he related to them not as underlings or cogs in a machine, but as people– people that he was on the same level with. When we relate to people with empathy and consideration, leadership becomes a question of relationship, not transaction, and not command. Instead, people follow us because we inspire trust and loyalty, and because we have demonstrated that we deserve the privilege of taking their wellbeing into our own hands. Empathy, then, is what distinguishes a true leader and conqueror from a dictator.

- If you're a leader in any capacity, resist the temptation to think of people in your team purely in terms of their work on the job. Proactively show an interest in their lives, and pay close attention to any needs that are

going unmet. Can you offer some support? Can you lighten someone's load if you see them struggling, or arrange a fun activity if it's been a tough week?
- Be generous with your time, energy, and resources. Think about leadership as a position that others grant you. Anyone can be formally and officially in charge, but a leader is someone who inspires trust and loyalty.
- If times get tough, double-down on your attentiveness to your staff or employees, rather than scrambling to cover your own bases. Show others that their wellbeing is your concern, and they will be loyal and look to you to guide them out of a crisis.

Jacob's story

Jacob was a doctor and a young man who had always considered himself a high achiever. He was accomplished and he knew what he wanted, and he had spent his life systematically pursuing his goals with determination and sheer force of will. So when he was unexpectedly taken to court one year for malpractice, it felt like his life was ending.

The trial was complex, high profile, and incredibly stressful, not to mention it took years to play out, causing significant stress to both Jacob and his wife. Jacob had an illustrious career, but his was a high-risk specialty, and despite every best effort, the case looked increasingly desperate. Jacob began the trial with cautious optimism that it would soon be resolved, but as the years passed and the investigation became more and more convoluted, Jacob began to lose confidence in himself.

Soon, it was all he could think about. Knowing that an aggrieved patient had made a serious complaint against him ate away at his sense of identity and pride. The regulatory bodies were going through his life with a fine tooth comb, and he began to grow suspicious and fearful that people had it out for him. He worried about money, about his job, about his reputation... everything seemed to be threatened.

Throughout this prolonged ordeal, however, Jacob failed to notice something important: he had utterly neglected his wife. Even though she had loyally stood by him, so great was his fear and desire to save himself that he scarcely noticed her–nor did he notice the increasing strain being placed on their marriage.

When his wife announced one day that she was considering divorce, Jacob felt blindsided. And yet, he would later say that this second disaster had actually been a wakeup call that helped snap him out of his unhealthy obsession with the first.

Overcome with fear, he lost sight of his commitment to his wife, and neglected their marriage–the only thing he really valued, at the end of the day. He had stopped being a team player. He was so tangled up in the unfolding disaster that he failed to recognize how it was costing him the woman he loved. At that moment he knew with crystal clarity: the mission had to change. He no longer cared about the trial. His new mission was to save his marriage, and get through the nightmare *together*, no matter what.

Fast forward ten years, and Jacob is no longer even practicing medicine. The episode is for him a distant memory and, if he is honest, a total failure. He lost money, jeopardized his business, incurred reputational damage, and alienated many of his colleagues. But from the wreckage of that failure he pulled out something precious: his marriage. It did not just survive, but it bloomed, and Jacob earnedlearned many hard lessons about what mattered most to him in life.

At the end of his life many decades later, he was fondly remembered as a devoted husband and father, a wise grandfather and a much-loved friend, a mentor and community leader. People spoke of his warmth, his generosity, his kindness.

By the time he died, only a few remembered that he had ever been a doctor.

Ernest Shackleton's conqueror mindset: "Chin up. Keep going. Let's stick together. Tough times don't last; tough people do."

Conqueror traits: Camaraderie and connection. Recalibration, endurance, optimism.

- Pay attention to the morale of your team, and work hard to inspire trust, friendship, and loyalty.
- Don't go down with a sinking ship. Know when to cut losses and pivot.
- Even in the face of grave danger, maintain your empathy for others.

Questions for reflection:

In what ways has my mission changed since I first embarked on it?

What do I need to do today to maintain my own and others' morale?

What attitude do I want to take to the adversity I am currently facing?

Sun Tzu

"The supreme art of war is to subdue the enemy without fighting."

- **Sun Tzu**

Sun Tzu (c. 544–496 BC), was a legendary Chinese general, strategist, and author of *The Art of War*, a book that revolutionized military strategy with its emphasis on intelligence, adaptability, and careful observation. For this reason, though Sun Tzu's work is on one level a work of military genius, it is also a psychological treatise about the nature of victory itself.

Sun Tzu's words continue to offer the modern world profound insights into true leadership, resilience, and artful decision-making. His writing was poetic and perennial, teaching readers throughout the generations to apply his lessons to everything in life. By valuing **preparation, harmony, and the avoidance of**

unnecessary conflict, Sun Tzu's insights continue to inspire leaders across domains, as well as ordinary people who are eager to conquer life's more mundane battles.

Conquerors fight, and they win. But Sun Tzu's approach was to show that sometimes, we win when we don't fight at all. Sun Tzu was arguably a philosopher first and foremost, and his attitude was that fighting was usually a last resort. If fighting was necessary, however, then it should always be undertaken deliberately and with careful forethought. This approach to battle is really a methodology, and an entirely different perspective towards conflict itself.

Little is known about Sun Tzu, and there is disagreement about when and where he was born, and about which parts of his life were fact, and which parts were legend and historical fiction. There are some historians who doubt he even existed at all. Nevertheless, there are some surviving stories and tales about the man, and, if true, they reveal much about his possible character.

One story explains how the King of Wu, Sun Tzu's employer, had one day set him an impossible task to test the veracity of his military theories. The king asked him to transform a harem of 180 concubines into an army of coherent, obedient soldiers. Immediately Sun Tzu split the group of concubines into two, then appointed as commanders for each group two women he knew were favored by the king.

Sun Tzu appointed himself their general, and began by giving an order to face right, but the concubines just giggled. Sun Tzu claimed that it was the two commanders' responsibility to make sure that every concubine under them understood the commands she was giving. He gave the command again, but the concubines continued to giggle. Sun Tzu ordered that the commanders–the favorite concubines–be executed for their failure to manage those under them. Despite the king's protests, this was done, and new concubines were assigned as commanders. What do you think happened next time Sun Tzu gave an order? The entire group obeyed flawlessly.

Sun Tzu's point here was that, when responsibility and culpability are strategically allocated in an army, the mission will always be carried out–even if it means going against the king's wishes. Not only did Sun Tzu successfully rise to the challenge and make obedient soldiers out of giggling concubines, but he also demonstrated a higher vision of strategy, i.e., that the management of soldiers during war is not a question of might or force, but of psychology. By assigning such a task, the king revealed his own lack of military insight, and his assumption that the strength of an army lies simply in the strength of its individual members.

While this story certainly seems cruel to us, chances are that it isn't true, but rather allegorical. In Sun Tzu's philosophy, war is less like a wrestling match and more like a game of chess. The principle demonstrated in this little tale seems to be that, although it may seem vicious to execute two commanders, what if in the long run it guarantees the survival of the entire army, and the preservation of countless other civilians? The wise military strategist is able to look that far ahead and consider the whole picture.

Aligning with the Tao

It's worth mentioning that much of the wisdom of *The Art of War* is not Sun Tzu's alone. The work was written within a particular context, and inspired by the Eastern concept of the *Tao* and *De*. The concept of the Tao is unfamiliar to the Western mind, but it can be defined as the flow of reality itself, and the single force underlying the natural order of the universe.

It is the Tao that maintains natural order, and if we live virtuously, i.e., in harmony with the Tao, our being is associated with *De*. We can think of De as a state of integration with the Tao, and serene wholeness with it. A moral, upright life, then, is one lived in peaceful accordance with fundamental universal flows, and a disastrous life is one lived in opposition.

Both Taoism and Confucianism–faith systems that were ubiquitous in Sun Tzu's time–uphold the concept of the Tao. In the context of war, battle can be seen as an expression of the natural flow of being, and a wise and insightful leader will understand how to move *with* the Tao, and thus achieve success. Therefore, whether it is better to advance or to retreat, to yield or to stand strong, to wait or to pounce, becomes a matter of knowing the Tao. This is perhaps why *The Art of War* doesn't stop at military strategy alone, but also includes advice for cooperation, peace, diplomacy, and the overall principles of governance for a sound state.

Today, *The Art of War* is still as popular as it's ever been and is found on the bookshelves of all the world's great leaders and thinkers. It was beloved by many subsequent Chinese emperors, and was even an influence for Mao's *Little Red Book*. Author Steven C. Combs compares the language of the Tao with Aristotelian rhetoric, saying warfare is "used as a metaphor for rhetoric, and that both are philosophically based arts [...] **Warfare is analogous to persuasion, as a battle for hearts and minds.**"

One could argue that China's striving to become a world superpower is informed to this day by the ancient strategic principles outlined in *The Art of War*. Today, the Chinese continue to value traditional thinkers like Sun Tzu and extend and modernize his wisdom to culture, business, public policy, and even sports. In the West, Sun Tzu has been revered by business leaders, CEOs, and motivational influencers, and has been on and off bestseller lists for decades.

Bringing wisdom to warfare

While it may be true that *The Art of War* has sometimes been only superficially grasped by a Western audience, it nevertheless offers valuable insight some 2500 years after it was first written. Sun Tzu taught that *intelligence beats sheer force every time*, and that the best way to win was to only go to war when you were assured of winning in the first place. War, then, really plays out in the forethought, and in the correct appraisal of the advantages of both one's own position, and the position of one's enemy–this also applies when we ourselves are our own enemy!

Knowledge is power, and a decision made rashly seldom works out. A good conqueror acknowledges his weaknesses and emotions, without letting that undermine a broader, more objective view of the situation, not just now, but as it may unfold into the future. If you can muster enough grace, tact, preparation, and careful strategy, you will never need to make any big, desperate moves, and you will certainly never be caught on the backfoot dealing with a situation you never anticipated.

For Sun Tzu, timing was everything, and the best action is the action that is taken at precisely the right time. In the same way that the practitioner of the martial art Judo uses his opponent's own force and momentum to destabilize him, Sun Tzu advocates shrewd use of your opportunities. On the other hand, we need discipline and patient restraint to lay low and wait if our position is not favorable.

Finally, *The Art of War* counsels us to be observant and to gain knowledge of both ourselves and our adversaries. The idea is to be in a continual process of observation, adjustment, observation, adjustment; eternally responsive to changing circumstances, i.e., flowing with the Tao. The more elegance we can find, the more unnecessary aggravation and conflict we avoid, and the more we spare our resources. Calculated, intelligent action is thus not just a way to triumph over adversaries, but an art form.

Know your terrain

Sun Tzu advises us to understand the environment we're in before taking rash action. A general won't lead an aggressive advance in a new and unfamiliar territory, and neither should you barge in with a new plan or idea until you know where you are, so to speak.

- Whether planning a family trip or starting a new hobby, take the time to understand the terrain—literal or metaphorical. If you're hosting a party, learn your guests' preferences and the best timing for activities. If it's a new skill, research what tools or techniques you need. By knowing the terrain, you set the stage for a smoother path and fewer surprises.

- Sun Tzu says, "There are roads which must not be followed, armies which must not be attacked, towns which must not be besieged, positions which must not be contested, commands of the sovereign which must not be obeyed." Before you embark on a new plan, run it through in your mind first to anticipate potential snags. It's better to encounter any serious problems in your imagination first, rather than to discover them once your actions have already committed you.
- If you're heading into a negotiation, do whatever you can to understand who you'll be talking to, what they value, what they're trying to accomplish, and, crucially, what they are likely to think of *you*. Anticipate their questions and objections, and prepare responses in advance.
- If you're launching a new business, slyly sample your competitor's products or services, and speak to potential customers about their experiences and preferences. Find out everything you can about the exact reasons other similar businesses have failed.

Adapt like water

The Tao tells us that *nature does not hurry, yet everything is accomplished*. When we move with the natural flow of being, we are in aligned harmony and can expect success and prosperity. To put this in more Western terms, we can say that it's important to be flexible and to continuously adapt to life's eternally unfolding currents.

It's a question of attitude. When change arises, we can allow ourselves to flow and move with it. "Brittle things break before they bend," so pay attention and notice if circumstances are requiring a little more bend from you. Life moves and changes constantly, and it's a foolish man who tries to vainly hold onto what is constantly moving away. Instead, see yourself as water and take the shape of the container you're in.

- Imagine you're planning an outdoor barbecue, but the weather takes a turn. Instead of canceling, shift the event indoors and create a cozy atmosphere with fairy lights and music. Similarly, if you're training for a marathon and an injury sidelines you, adapt by focusing on recovery and cross-training.
- If you're feeling stressed, overwhelmed, confused, exhausted, or angry about how a situation is developing, resist the urge to, well, resist, and instead go quiet in yourself. Ask: Might at least some of your discomfort

be coming from your unwillingness to go with changes that are inevitable? Might you still be able to achieve your general aim even while giving up any specific ideas of how you should get there?

- Always remember that you can choose not to act, not to respond, not to even have an opinion. Sometimes inaction is the superior move if that inaction is wise and carefully considered. For example, when dealing with the demands of someone rash and impulsive, it's often wisest to be nonreactive–if you are patient, the consequences of their own actions may resolve the issue for you, and you will have spared yourself unnecessary aggravation.

Choose your battles

A military leader surveys a complex field of possibility. There are hundreds, if not thousands, of men, countless possibilities, scores of different ways for the story to unfold. How does he decide on a path of action? In *The Art of War*, Sun Tzu describes a field throughout which battle is flowing and interacting with different elements:

Goals: Decide what is ultimately of importance and have a clear understanding of why it is important (this will allow you to stay focused and able to adjust if necessary).

Outside forces: We are all living and acting inside a grand theatre called reality. What is the arrangement of factors and influences outside of our control? This can be literal things like the weather, but also includes any and all external conditions you find yourself in.

The plan: You need something concrete to execute in the real world, in real time, and you need this plan to be responsive to change. This means there need to be back-up plans and alternative solutions.

The commander: That's you! How effective you are at commanding the elements under your control (whatever or whoever they may be) comes down to your virtue, i.e., your alignment with the great Tao.

The way: This is the method and the manner in which you enact your plan. Victory is not just a rough tally of winners and losers, but a *style*. You can conduct yourself with fear and force and clumsiness, or you can govern a situation with poise, control, and wisdom.

- Survey your current situation, whatever it may be, big or small, short- or long-term. Then consider each of the above elements and how they might interact. For example, given your goals and your plan to achieve that goal, what is the best way to conduct yourself? How might outside forces

interfere? In what ways can the plan be changed if there is interference?
- If outside forces are truly against you and the plan won't work, accept that the wisest choice may be to simply wait. If you have thoroughly surveyed your field of possibility and can see no way at all for you to advance your plan, don't lose hope. You can defer your goals, adjust them, or even change them entirely. No matter what happens, remind yourself that *you* are the commander.
- Not every battle is worth fighting, and knowing when to let go is power. If a friend forgets your birthday but later shows genuine regret, consider whether the energy of confrontation outweighs the value of the relationship. Similarly, if a neighbor's noisy dog bothers you, but their kindness in other ways strengthens community ties, weigh your options. By focusing on battles that align with your deeper goals, you save energy for the victories that truly count.

Ben's story

Ben was in the difficult position of having to fire an employee that he personally liked. A certain situation had devolved to an extent that letting this employee go was probably the only way forward, and yet Ben was nervous about creating more ill will and leaving the employee with a taste for legal retribution.

On one hand, Ben held all the cards and knew that he was in the legal right to dismiss this employee. On the other hand, he was also keenly aware that the company was not in any position to waste resources fighting this employee, and the situation that precipitated his dismissal was ongoing and pretty delicate. In short, he did not want to further inflame any upset–both for this employee and for existing employees who had made complaints against him. Yet he also knew that the dismissal needed to happen.

Though a colleague had advised him to handle the entire mess briefly and with cool professionalism, Ben decided on a different tactic. He hated the idea of "crushing his enemies" and had always been uneasy leveraging power dynamics and manipulating people. So, he waited a little while. He thought things over carefully. Then he chose his moment and approached the employee at a non-stressful time of the employee's own choosing. He politely and clearly made it known that the company did indeed hold the strategically stronger position, but he would not insult the employee's intelligence by brandishing this fact with force or aggression.

What Ben did was to refrain from firing the employee at all. Instead, he outlined the situation as he saw it, and offered the employee the option to resign with minimal fuss and reasonable compensation. Without realizing it,

Ben had followed Sun Tzu's advice to "build a golden bridge for your enemy to retreat on." The truth was that Ben's company could technically overpower and dominate the employee and *force* him out. But doing this would waste unnecessary resources–on both sides. It was excessive, when both he and the employee were aware of the power imbalance, and were similarly reluctant to get embroiled in costly and exhausting legal battles.

Ben had been vaguely aware that this was a common strategy for avoiding litigation, but it wasn't until he was in that position himself that he understood that such a tactic is also about preserving mental and emotional resources, not just financial ones. He was in fact helping the employee to save face (a common Confucian principle) and to soften the humiliation of defeat. The "bridge" in this case is golden because it offers the employee a way out that doesn't diminish his dignity or lower his self-esteem. It is an invitation, offered with diplomacy and good etiquette.

The employee made a pretense of reluctantly weighing up his options, but quickly agreed to Ben's terms. And just like that, the battle was won before it had really started. Had Ben gone in "guns blazing" and brandishing the company's full force, he would only have inspired defensiveness in his "opponent" and they both would have spent themselves on pointless combat. What's more, Ben might have earned a reputation for burning bridges and making enemies–and why risk that? Ben understood that day what it really means to pick your battles, and exactly what Sun Tzu meant when he advised "subduing one's enemy without fighting."

Sun Tzu's conqueror mindset: "To the mind that is still, the whole universe surrenders."

Conqueror traits: Wisdom, harmony, strategy, deliberation, intelligence over force.

- The best war is one that never takes place. Be strategic, be flexible, and make small, deliberate movements to achieve your purpose.
- Knowledge is power. Know yourself and your enemy.
- Choose your battles carefully, and never let rash emotion get the better of you.
- When the correct posture is adopted, there is no conflict.

Questions for reflection:

What do I still need to observe, learn, or understand about the "terrain" I'm in?

What kind of a person do I need to be to adapt to the changes I see unfolding around me?

Does the battle that I'm facing actually need to be fought?

Joan of Arc

"Faith is taking the first step even when you don't see the whole staircase."

- **Martin Luther King, Jr.**

In this chapter, we will learn of a person with such strength and bravery that she completely shatters conventional understandings of what it really means to be a *conqueror*. The great heroic figures we have discussed so far have all fit a certain predictable mold: they are seasoned warriors, empire builders, and military leaders. These, we are told, are the Great Men and Women of History, and their accomplishments are humanity's best standard for leadership.

The story of Joan of Arc is a refreshing reminder that there are many ways to conquer, many formidable weapons to yield, and many ways to be called on to serve, to fight, and to triumph. Joan of Arc's story is so fascinating because it speaks to the **power of conviction and how real strength can emerge from what the world considers the most unlikely source.** After all, Joan was a teenage girl, a mere illiterate peasant, and had precisely zero military or diplomatic training. She was, to conventional standards, a nobody.

And yet, whatever Joan of Arc *did* possess, it allowed her to persuade the crown prince of Valois to put her at the head of the French army, and lead the siege against Orléans. It also allowed her to win a dazzling victory, and to keep on winning victories even after her death. So lasting was Joan of Arc's impression on the French psyche, that she is to this day cherished as a great martyr, leader, and patron saint of France.

Joan's early life was humble. She was born in 1412 to poor tenant farmers in northeastern France and was raised with a deep and abiding love for the Catholic faith. She had been born in the very heart of the Hundred Years' War, and her homeland had long been occupied by the English. The French Crown Prince was disinherited in 1420, and England's Henry V was made to rule over France, with his son Henry VI succeeding him in 1422.

When Joan was around 13 years old, she heard the voice of God, who told her she was being given a vast and sacred mission: to save France and restore her to her rightful king. It's hard, even now, to imagine what had gone on in the heart and mind of this young peasant girl, but Joan's conviction did not falter for a moment. Despite her father urging her to marry, Joan resisted and instead made a vow of chastity; she knew she was destined for something else.

In 1428, when Joan was just 16, she travelled to Vaucouleurs to seek an audience with Charles VII, the man who would later be crowned king. The young girl faced considerable opposition, yet she also quickly gathered a loyal group of followers. At the time there had been something of a local prophecy that foretold that a young virgin would appear to save France and give her victory; the persistent Joan convinced those that gathered around her that she was this promised leader.

Joan insistently requested the local magistrate Robert de Baudricourt to give her an audience with the prince; when he eventually relented and agreed to arrange an interview, Joan immediately cut off her hair, donned male dress, and embarked on the 11 day journey through enemy territory, to the crown prince's palace at Chinon. When the young Joan met the crown prince, she told him in all confidence that he would be crowned king, if he would raise an army for her to march on Orléans and take it back from the English.

Exactly what transpired in the conversation between the young Joan and the crown prince is a mystery. It was said, however, that the girl had revealed information that she could have known only if she had indeed been sent by God–she knew about the prayer that Baudricourt himself had made to God to save his country. Despite every one of his counsellors strongly advising against it, the crown prince did as Joan requested. In 1429 Joan set off, leading her army on a white horse, wearing gleaming armor, and brandishing a flag.

Joan was defiant and self-assured. She led multiple successful attacks in the Siege of Orléans, and conquered any resisting town that stood in her path. Joan and her loyal followers personally escorted the crown prince to Reims to be coronated as King Charles VII later that year, and her reputation was secured.

Joan, however, was not done. She wanted to press on and re-capture Paris, too, but Charles himself was reluctant, and uneasy about her growing authority. In 1430, Charles ordered retaliation for the Burgundian attack on Compiège, and Joan led the defense. There the Burgundians captured her, took her to the castle of Bouvreuil (which was occupied by the English) and sentenced her to a trial.

She was made to answer to 70 charges, including accusations that she was a sorceress and witch, a cross-dresser, a heretic, and a fraud. In truth, the charges were a political ploy to remove the young Joan and thereby discredit Charles. As for the king himself, he followed the advice of his counsellors and distanced himself from Joan, and made no attempt to rescue her. She remained in custody for a year, before being forced into a confession that she had indeed never heard the word of God.

Just when it appeared that she would be spared and released, however, she once again flagrantly put on men's clothing, and so in 1432, aged just 19 years old, she was sentenced to death once and for all, and burnt at the stake.

Twenty years later, Charles VII ordered a retrial, and her name was formally cleared. In 1909 she was beatified by Pope Pius X with a statue in Notre Dame Cathedral, and then in 1920, Pope Benedict XV canonized her as a saint and a martyr. It had taken more than 500 years, but Joan's fame had grown to mythic proportions. Joan had received visions and she *was* a vision: a young, brave girl with a banner, riding a white horse. For an entire nation this image became an icon for righteous victory, courage, and piety.

What can we make of this remarkable legend of the virgin on the white horse?

Joan's was a life of faith

Many leadership gurus today will emphasize the importance of having confidence, self-belief, and faith in what you want to achieve. The fact is, Joan of Arc had something much better than that. Having been raised in humility, Joan understood the power of *submission to a higher purpose*. Joan's destiny was not for ultimate personal greatness or valor, but for the victory of her nation and the triumph of her faith. She heard the voice of God *and she listened*.

It's difficult to imagine just how much trust in this voice she must have had. If the story had happened today, it would be as though an uneducated, working-class teenage girl had set her mind to not only converse directly with the president of her country, but to convince him to let her lead one of the most important and decisive battles in the nation's history. Such a feat today seems nearly impossible, and perhaps it seemed even more impossible in Joan's day; and yet, the girl herself was undaunted.

Today, Joan of Arc is lauded as a defender of France, a patron saint and one of the most studied figures from the Middle Ages. But way back in 1425, before any victories had been won and before the world knew her name, she was simply a 13-year-old girl. She testified to having seen visions of Saint Michael, a defender of Fance and the patron saint of her hometown, Domrémy. She also claimed to see visions of St. Catherine of Alexandria, and St. Margaret of Antioch, both virgin saints who fought and prevailed against powerful forces and were martyred for their cause.

Today, explanations for these visions have been numerous. Scholars claim that Joan might have suffered from epilepsy, a brain tumor, hysteria, schizophrenia, ergot poisoning and plain old delusion instilled by a strongly religious upbringing. Indeed, rural 1400s France was steeped in piety and superstition, and Marie Robine of Avignon, a French mystic, had made prophesies that a virgin with a banner would save France. Was Joan of Arc *really* destined by God to do what she did? Did she *really* receive visions?

What is important, perhaps, is not what did or did not happen, but rather the heart and mind of the young woman who had the determination within herself to follow her conviction, no matter what. She did not give up, and she did not entertain doubters. She believed so strongly in her divine mission that she had no qualms appealing to Baudricourt, again and again, despite his harsh and repeated refusals. **His disbelief in her never became doubt in herself. She *knew* what she had been destined for, and that was all.**

Her ability to maintain such certainty in the face of constant opposition inspired those around her and became the cornerstone of her remarkable leadership. **She did not lead by might, or intelligence, or cunning, but by simple faith that never, ever wavered**. When it comes to leadership, there can sometimes be a sense that great effort and striving are required. In Joan's case, her leadership was founded in her spirit and conviction.

Charles is said to have requested his most trusted church elders to interview her, and they reported that she was a woman of humility, chastity, and virtue. Joan was *not* driven by personal ambition at all, but by her own core values and sincerity to live a virtuous life. In the modern world, where it often seems that success is only available to those who possess a certain ruthlessness and cunning, Joan of Arc's example reminds us of the real power of *sincerity*.

An authentic leader, driven by ideals higher than their own pride and vanity, is infinitely more trustworthy, and inspires loyal followers. Joan did not request permission when it came to morals. She did not seek validation from others, but took her purpose from God. She did not negotiate and compromise with the world around her; she simply moved ahead with courageous indifference, charting a course revealed to her through her own faith.

Finally, this was a young girl who did not shy away from taking action. She led by example and was at the front lines, ready to do for her country precisely what she had asked her dedicated followers to do. Unlike those who direct troops from a distance, and who play with tactics and diplomacy as though merely playing a game, Joan was hands-on and committed, and this earned her the love and admiration of her troops–many of whom had no belief in her to start. She was not content being a mere figurehead; she donned the necessary armor and galloped into the fray herself.

Your core beliefs are your anchor

It hardly matters whether you share Joan of Arc's faith or not. **What does matter, however, is what faith you *do* have, and its strength.** Joan's faith was enough to carry her through unspeakable adversity; it was enough to keep her strong despite the accusations of others; it was enough to not only overcome the doubts of an entire army of soldiers who had no faith in her, but to inspire love and devotion in those same soldiers. Most of us can only hope to have faith that strong!

Knowing what you stand for is a way to set down an anchor. Your core beliefs, your values, and your convictions are what will keep you going when everything else falters. However, it's not enough to identify vague preferences. Rather, **faith is the ability to hold strong to the things you value even when there is no proof, and no external validation.**

A leader takes the risk of completely believing in a vision they have seen, even while they know that others have not seen that vision. Followers will demand evidence, and ask for explanations, and seek out guarantees and assurances. But a leader must take those first few crucial steps alone, and they have to do it on pure faith. It's precisely this that enables them to conquer; when they can first conquer their own fear and doubt, they can go out and win even the most unlikely battles, so to speak.

Again, values go beyond mere preference, habit, or personality. Your values are something that you are willing to fight for, and to sacrifice for. They are the things that you would cling to even if nobody else in the world agreed that they mattered. In fact, they are the things you couldn't help but believe in, even if you were persecuted and attacked because of that belief.

Granted, this is a high bar. Often, deep conviction comes with an enormous cost. Joan of Arc was executed and did not even live to 20 years old. She gave her entire life for what she believed, and all the honor and glory she received came hundreds of years after her vicious execution. Following what you believe even when you are alone in that belief is not easy. Then again, true conquerors are not primarily interested in ease, or in validation and approval from others–especially from those who themselves lack anchoring in any sincere faith.

Take a moment to contemplate your values and core beliefs–the very deepest ones–and be honest with yourself. Are you are in need of more courage in living up to those values? If you are having trouble identifying your values, journal or meditate on the following prompts and questions:

- What actions or principles have you always stuck with throughout life, no matter what? Think about the activities you pursued even when you didn't have the time and you weren't paid to do it. Think about those things that you almost can't help but do and inquire into the deeper values behind those actions.
- Think about the values your heroes and role models have, as those values may reflect your own.
- On the other hand, what about the people who have lived lives you consider unworthy, dishonorable, unprincipled, etc.? Be curious about the inverse of their values.
- Think back to the past and see if you can remember a time you felt deeply fulfilled and satisfied in yourself. What had you done? *How* had you done it? And why? This deep feeling of being intentional points directly to your core values and convictions, even if it's only a memory of something small and fleeting.
- Finally, ask yourself what you and you alone bring to the table. Each of us is unique, and possesses a completely individual set of skills, perspectives, and abilities. What are yours? How might they speak to your higher purpose in the world?

Transform doubt into momentum

You may be "called" several times to pursue a dream or ambition. Perhaps you have a business idea that won't leave you, a yearning to build or create something new, or a hunger to learn, to serve, or even to defend, much like Joan of Arc. Few of us will ever feel called to rescue an entire nation, but the calls we do hear, and the visions we do see, are no less important just because they're smaller in scale.

Sadly, many of us hear the call over and over again, but ignore it. Or we take a leap of faith and make the first move, only to be thoroughly discouraged at the very first obstacle. We may apply to do a course, be hired onto a job, or be accepted into a program only to be rejected again and again. We may try to launch a new idea, or put our creations out into the world, only to immediately retreat again when we are met with opposition.

But consider this. Joan of Arc's story has now been told all over the world for hundreds of years. In every retelling, we are told how persistent she was. She kept on asking, she kept on pushing, and she never stopped pleading her case. These details are included in the story for a reason: they make Joan's ultimate triumph even more amazing. They point to her strength and faith. They are evidence of her conviction, and that evidence is precisely what makes people fall in love with her tale of victory, regardless of nationality.

In other words, obstacles are an intrinsic part of a conqueror's story. They are not hurdles that get in the way of the hero's arc; they are the very conditions that ensure that the hero's prize at the end is actually worth winning or achieving.

Natural conquerors like Joan of Arc do not see obstacles like other people do. Without conviction and faith, you are subject to the stronger will and intention of other people. That means that if they tell you that you can't do it, you instantly concur, and you stop trying. For a conqueror, however, other people's resistance, objection, and judgment are certainly difficult, but they never seem as *significant*. Such objections and obstacles are seen as annoying, but they are no reason to doubt your course for even a second.

Joan of Arc faced countless obstacles, but she never felt personally picked on by fate, or unfairly hindered. The burden was never too heavy. **It's easy to think that if we really are fated by God and set out on a divine mission, then everything should be easy for us. But this is an illusion.** The greater the ambition, the more obstacles there will be, even if you are on precisely the path you should be, doing everything you need to.

If you are dealing with gatekeepers, asking for help, or trying to pitch projects and ideas, work hard to never allow any obstacles to discourage you. Refine your approach, then try again. You may need to make changes or seek out those people best able to support your vision, but either way, remind yourself that struggles are normal and to be expected.

- If an initial attempt doesn't work, then *immediately* take action to plan your next step, rather than dwelling on the setback itself. Acknowledge the obstacle but don't get fixated on it, and instead keep moving forward. Ask, "If that didn't work, what *will* work?"
- Don't be shy. You may need to be a little forceful as you present yourself. Remember again that even though you have deep conviction in something yourself, you still might need to work hard to convince others.
- Don't take things personally. People will obstruct you for all sorts of reasons that have nothing to do with you. When someone says you can't do something, they are expressing to you *their own* fears and limits–you do not have to accept those fears and limits for yourself.

Be visible in your commitments

Today, you can find countless artworks depicting Joan of Arc riding at the head of her troops as she led them in battle, banner waving magnificently.

Whether Joan understood her role as a figurehead and inspiration is not clear, but this is nevertheless what she was. **The young woman inspired respect, trust, and admiration because she was so completely and thoroughly identified with her purpose**. By cutting her hair, donning armor, and "suiting up" for her life's mission, she communicated iron-clad commitment to her purpose without saying a word.

For many of us, however, it can sometimes feel almost impossible to be such a visible champion for our causes and beliefs. We may shrink back, keep quiet, and play small, even as we yearn internally to do something bigger and braver. Sadly, our most cherished ambitions and plans can fizzle away in private, and we miss out on opportunities to speak our message, to rally others, and to lead them towards the things we believe in.

It was Joan's *presence* on the battlefield that inspired her troops, along with what she stood for. In your own life, you may find that you need to drum up the courage to be more present to your own cause:

- If you are going against norms and conventions, being very visible can feel risky-so start small. Can you organize a small event or host a project or meetup in line with your values and goals? Can you volunteer for something?

- Try to speak up and share with others all the things that fire you up, and don't hold back your enthusiasm out of fear of offending. Joan's conviction was able to persuade princes and magistrates and soldiers to her cause. Don't underestimate the power of just showing up and speaking your truth.
- Finally, if you hope to inspire and lead others, think carefully about the higher ideals that speak to people's hearts and minds. Joan succeeded, not on her own platform, but on lofty principles like justice and patriotism. Her entire image spoke of this, so that she herself became a symbol of her purpose. How might you become a more accurate spokesperson for *your* cause, for example, in the way you dress or present yourself?

Natalie's story

Natalie was also a young girl of humble circumstances. Her story is much smaller than Joan of Arc's, but it contains significant impact. One day, when Natalie was just 10 years old, she saw a group of bullies picking on a younger classmate who had a significant facial deformity. As the bullies mocked the younger boy, Natalie felt herself burnt up with anger and injustice. She remembers how, in that moment, she felt irresistibly compelled to do something.

She marched up to the bullies and proceeded to defend the younger boy. A crowd of curious students had started to gather around the incident as Natalie bravely castigated the bullies with a ferociousness she didn't know she had. But to everyone's surprise, the young boy, feeling humiliated at needing to be rescued by a *girl*, instantly turned on her too, and began to tease and mock her efforts. The bullies joined in, and so did the onlookers, and Natalie's high-minded attempt at justice backfired. She had made herself the target for jeering and derision.

Natalie ran off that day, and her reputation at school never quite recovered. Eventually everyone grew up and more than forty years later Natalie encountered an old classmate–someone who remembered observing the incident. Natalie recalled with sadness how she had been ganged up on, and how pointless it had been to stand up for what was right. The other classmate was mystified. "What do you mean? We all thought that what you did was amazing. I've always felt so much regret for not standing up for you, and for being so cowardly. We were just stupid kids. But *you* did the right thing, and I've always admired you for it."

The right thing is always the right thing, whether other people can see it or not.

Joan of Arc's conqueror mindset: "I am not afraid. I was born to do this."

Conqueror traits: Purpose, conviction, humility, self-sacrifice.

- Anchor yourself in your faith, your values, and your deepest convictions.
- Don't take setbacks and obstacles personally. Persist. Just because you are destined for something doesn't mean it will be easy or instant.
- Fully identify yourself with your mission, and commit to what you stand for.

Questions for reflection:

Am I fully connected to a purpose greater than myself?

What are the things I am willing to sacrifice my life, my time, my resources for?

Is there a personal conviction I need to speak more openly and plainly to the world?

Alexander the Great

"Through every generation of the human race there has been a constant war, a war with fear. Those who have the courage to conquer it are made free and those who are conquered by it are made to suffer until they have the courage to defeat it, or death takes them."

- **Alexander the Great**

Alexander the Great remains a towering figure in history, revered for his military genius, vision, and transformative leadership. By the age of just 32, he had forged one of the largest empires the world had ever known, spanning from the Balkans to India, and from Egypt to Armenia. Known for fighting alongside his men and leading from the front, Alexander combined physical prowess, strategic brilliance, and unrelenting ambition to shape history and inspire generations after him. Even other notable great men, like Julius Caesar and Napolean Bonaparte, considered him a role model and strove to emulate his mental dexterity, conviction, and oratory genius.

Most of us have heard of Alexander the Great, but what made him so great, anyway? Alexander III was born around 356 BC Pella in the Kingdom of Macedon (the ancestral home of Cleopatra). Alexander's father was king of Macedon, Philip II, and his mother was Olympias, a favorite of the king's seven or eight wives.

The ancient historian Plutarch claims that the night before her wedding, Olympia dreamt that a thunderbolt struck her womb and created a fire that spread far and wide into the world. It was said that King Philip had a vision of sealing his wife's womb with the image of a lion–an indication that the boy's real parent had been none other than the god Zeus himself. Other myths held that on the day of his birth, certain momentous battles were won and the temple of Artemis and Ephesus burnt down–because the goddess Artemis herself was not there but instead attending the boy's birth. The veracity of these myths aside, such legends indicate that even before his birth, there was gravity and valor attached to the young Alexander's fate.

Alexander was given a classical education and was tutored by the great Aristotle, who taught him about philosophy, mathematics, medicine, rhetoric, logic, and art. Together they read

Euripeds and Homer, all in the Temple of the Nymphs. He could play musical instruments, hunt, wrestle, ride horses, and recite lyric poetry. Stories of the youth's strength and ambition abounded, and the boy soon acquired a reputation for near superhuman ability.

Alexander was no pampered aristocrat, however, and his honors, though obviously inflated, were still roundly based in his astonishing military record. The battle at Granicus River was arguably the most crucial event of his life and was the moment that the youth's fateful prominence really began. Alexander was just 22, but already a king and a general. He was facing the Persian army–superior in many ways–and he was unproven in battle. Despite being young, inexperienced, and on the back foot, Alexander led with bravado and decisiveness that ensured a momentous victory. To this day, historians and military strategists marvel at the way the young Alexander read his opponent and outsmarted the Persian assault.

He had proven his mettle and had cemented his role as a legitimate and rightful king and commander. In battle. he engaged in brutal hand-to-hand combat, sustaining serious injuries and fighting fiercely before his soldier's very own eyes, winning both their loyalty and their admiration. Alexander's kudos as a military genius rested forever more on his ability to forge trusting relationships with his men. He would not be a remote, distant ruler, but right there on the frontlines, fighting side by side with his army.

Alexander's earliest campaigns were an attempt to cement his position in Greece, then expand East, crossing the Hellespont into Anatolia, and subduing the Persian forces at the Battle of Granicus. From his Macedonian base, he conquered vast territories spanning right across the Persian Empire. One battle and siege at a time, he captured and defeated Syria, Egypt, Mesopotamia, and the Indus River regions in what are today known as Afghanistan and Pakistan.

The battles at Issus and Gaugamela were decisive. Alexander overthrew the Persian king Darius III, and brought the region under his control, ushering in a new Hellenistic period of fruitful cultural exchange between Greece and the East. After securing Persia, Alexander marched into Egypt, where he was welcomed as a liberator and founded the city of Alexandria. Throughout his career, Alexander displayed military prowess marked by innovative tactics, bold action, and confident leadership that inspired, rather than subjugated, his troops, leading to a legacy as one of history's greatest military commanders.

Alexander would, like many golden era heroes of the same time period, come to be seen as more of a god than a king. His story is of such glory, conquest, and valor that it fits comfortably beside those of the mythical Achilles and the other heroes of classical antiquity. Truly, he has attained a kind of immortality, and his story lives on to inspire others to his day.

And yet, in other ways, Alexander's real genius was in his ability to connect as a man to this fellow man, and to fight with them in the trenches, so to speak. The enigmatic Alexander, who lamented the fact that there was only one world for him to conquer, also said, "Whatever possession we gain by our sword cannot be sure or lasting, but the love gained by kindness and moderation is certain and durable."

Slicing through the Gordian Knot

Inspired by figures like Achilles, Alexander's ambition was limitless, epitomized by his audacious handling of the proverbial "Gordian Knot." The legend explains how Alexander brought his army to Gordium, the capital city of Phrygia (Turkey today), where he was presented with the chariot of Gordius, the city's founder. The chariot was tied to a pole with a hopelessly complex knot. Legend had it that a seer had prophesied that the one who could untie the knot would be ruler of all Asia. Approaching the knot, Alexander could at first not work it loose, but then simply drew his sword and sliced through it with a single stroke.

This neat little legend is a poignant illustration of how swift, decisive action is often what's really needed. Alexander chose bold action over hesitation—he decided to solve the problem on his own terms and declared the knot undone. This decisive approach not only characterized his ongoing strategy, but also rallied his followers to believe in achieving the impossible.

There is a kind of concrete, tangible charisma to this approach to problem-solving, and it's Alexander's directness that inspired both trust and courage. He was certainly an intelligent strategist and thinker, but he also understood the raw power of action–he got his hands dirty and he *did* things. Ancient sources describe a man who was dedicated to physical training and was fit and strong, leading his men with stamina and agility. Alexander was no soft-handed bureaucrat or politician or academic, but a warrior king molded according to the classical Greek image.

Take bold, fearless, direct action to solve problems

Alexander once said, "Each moment free from fear makes a man immortal."

They are certainly arresting words. **To act with decisiveness and boldness means we need to be greater than all those fears and anxieties that would convince us to be hesitant.** Much ink has been spilled about Alexander's exploits, but two things are crystal clear: He was *never* shy and retiring, and he did not second-guess himself.

How can we possibly emulate such confidence in our own lives? The trick is to refuse to succumb to fear. If we negotiate with our fear and allow it to delay and confuse us, we are essentially wasting time battling ourselves. Instead, slice through your mental knots and carry on. Overthinkers, procrastinators, and perfectionists can spend their lives fretting over the proverbial knot, carefully planning a strategy to (one day) carefully pick it loose...

While care and prudence are sometimes wise, often the problem is that we are in our own way, and we simply need to *act*. At the root of our indecision may lie plain old fear-fear that we lack the ability, fear of repercussions, fear of failure, fear of success. The idea is not to overthink it, and not to let problems and tangles dictate to you; rather, remember that the solution will likely not be on the knot's terms!

- Instead of trying to organize every shelf meticulously, grab a few boxes and ruthlessly declutter, donating anything you haven't touched in a year. Or, if you've been procrastinating a heartfelt apology to a friend, pick up the phone right now and say, "I've been meaning to call—I'm sorry." Don't waste time stewing and planning and second-guessing. Just do something. By

cutting through hesitation, you can tackle problems head-on and free yourself from unnecessary stress.
- Get your hands dirty. Rather than standing aloof from conflicts or problems, get involved, speak plainly, and take action without angst. If you're at work and your colleagues are fretting about a certain problem, don't join them in fretting; instead, get to work solving it then and there. You do not need permission or validation from others to shine, and you don't need to explain yourself; if you have the answer, be bold and take action.
- Try to think of any areas in your life right now where you are hesitating. Chances are, there's some kind of fear holding you back. Rather than psychoanalyzing the fear, however, commit today to taking a single, tiny step in the right direction. Take a risk, share your feelings, make a bold request, or draw a line. You may find that the relief of proactive movement is so much greater than the illusion of security you may have felt in inaction.

Identify your "empire"

Alexander said,

> *"If it were not my purpose to combine barbarian things with things Hellenic, to traverse and civilize every continent, to search out the uttermost parts of land and*

> *sea, to push the bounds of Macedonia to the farthest Ocean, and to disseminate and shower the blessings of the Hellenic justice and peace over every nation, I should not be content to sit quietly in the luxury of idle power, but I should emulate the frugality of Diogenes. But as things are, forgive me Diogenes, that I imitate Herakles, and emulate Perseus, and follow in the footsteps of Dionysos, the divine author and progenitor of my family, and desire that victorious Hellenes should dance again in India and revive the memory of the Bacchic revels among the savage mountain tribes beyond the Kaukasos..."*

Alexander's conquest of the Persian Empire was fueled by his unwavering belief in his destiny to unify vast territories. His intention was to take his place among the gods themselves, and his realm would be nothing less than the known world–every continent, every nation. His aim was not mere personal victory, wealthy, or glory, but the vindication of his entire ancestral line, and a reshaping of the whole earth according to the glorious Greek design...

Phew! Must we really be *that* ambitious to learn from Alexander the Great? Of course not. And yet, if we identify and commit ourselves to our own deeply held and meaningful goals, we too have an "empire" of our own. Ambition is not really about scale or size. It's about unwavering conviction, and applying ourselves to achieve our own chosen ends, no matter what. What those ends are is up to us.

Alexander really would conquer the world in more or less the way he had intended, but even he had to do it one step at a time. Even he was not called "The Great" when he was still young and had not yet won his first battle. In the same way, our ambitions will be achieved step by step, one battle at a time.

- Say you've always dreamed of running a marathon, but you've never jogged a mile. Start small—commit to running for 10 minutes three times a week, then gradually increase. Break the goal into pieces, like signing up for a local 5K, finding the perfect pair of shoes, or joining a running group. Your marathon isn't just a race; it's proof you can conquer your limits.
- Identify your priorities and be crystal clear about what you will *not* spend time on. Alexander was great, but not at everything; his personal life, for instance, was mediocre. Though he did eventually marry (three times) and have a child, the historian Curtius claimed that he "scorned sensual pleasures" and many assumed he was a homosexual. The point is that he had identified his empire–world domination–and domestic life was simply not a priority.

- Not many of us can be said to have been fathered by Zeus himself, but all of us have values, deeply held beliefs, and passions that we are willing to fight for. What might you be "born to do"? Are you a born artist, friend, businessman, storyteller, father, builder, or peacemaker? What set of skills were you born with? Stake a claim on *that* empire – regardless of how big that territory is.

Lead from the front

Alexander didn't just demand effort; he inspired it by enduring the exact same hardships as his soldiers. Imagine you're helping your family move houses. Instead of standing aside, directing where the boxes should go, you're the first to carry the heaviest load—lugging your grandma's antique dresser up three flights of stairs or staying late to unpack the kitchen so it's usable by morning. Your willingness to take on the hardest tasks inspires everyone else to follow suit, and suddenly, the dreaded move feels less overwhelming because they know you've got their back. You've become a leader, and you've thought–and behaved–like a true conqueror.

- If you find yourself constantly complaining how something isn't right, or how "someone needs to do something," then challenge yourself to be that someone. Instead of complaining that there are no salsa groups in your neighborhood, for example, set one up yourself. If a communal gate near your house needs to be fixed, just fix it.

- If you manage a team, never ask them to take risks or incur costs that you haven't already shown yourself willing to take. If overtime is required, show up on evenings and weekends right along with them. If you make cuts to bonuses, make sure yours is the first to go.
- You must be willing to do things today others won't do, in order to have the things tomorrow others won't have. Go above and beyond without waiting to be asked and surround yourself with people who take pride in hard work and diligence. Whatever you do, do it *excellently*. Even if it's only a summer job, take the initiative, be bold, and do it well.

Eric's story

Eric had just graduated as an elementary school teacher, and was eager to get off on the right foot with his new class. However, one student–Alex–proved immediately that he intended to be an ongoing challenge. This young boy was disruptive, unruly, and wildly disobedient. He was notorious with the other teachers, who had largely given up on him, and who had advised Eric to do the same.

But something about this approach did not sit right with Eric. Though others scoffed at his idealism and inexperience, Eric loved children and felt that he was born to support them, and nurture their learning. He didn't just want to teach; he wanted to be one of those amazing teachers that people talk about with reverence and love well into adulthood. He wanted to be a truly exceptional teacher. To do that, he would need to establish himself in this school, and over this class. And to do that, he would need to neutralize the young boy's "threat" and bring him over to his side.

One afternoon, during a particularly challenging lesson on fractions, Alex began loudly humming a rude pop song, clearly intending to distract his classmates. Eric could quickly see that chaos would take over if he didn't act. Without thinking, he casually strolled over to Alex's desk and started humming along, incorporating the melody of the song into his explanation of fractions.

As Eric sang loudly and confidently over the class, the students laughed with surprise, but very quicky a hush fell over everyone as they paid close attention. Alex appeared to be the most intently focused of all, hanging on to every word that came out of Eric's mouth... and singing along. Alex had realized the song was now a tool to understand the math concept, and soon, the whole class was quietly humming along, engaged in the lesson. Instead of disrupting the class, the boy was now proudly leading it–under Eric's guidance. Eric had endeared himself to the rebellious boy while still taking firm control of the situation and steering everyone towards what mattered: the lesson.

With bold, decisive action, Eric had redirected the student's energy and from that day on, little Alex was far less interested in disrupting the class. In fact, young Alex felt a growing kinship with his teacher and deep loyalty towards him, because he had not given up on him like other teachers had, nor had he been easily scared off by his bad behavior. Had Eric hesitated on that day, however, he may have lost control of the classroom as well as lost the respect of the boy. Instead, he gradually built up a more trusting relationship with Alex and the class. Eric lead from the front, met his students where they were, and faced the challenge head on, with swiftness and boldness.

Alexander the Great's conqueror mindset: "Fortune favors the brave. And I was born to be brave."

Conqueror traits: Boldness, fearlessness, swiftness, decisive action, leadership, focused priorities.

- Be bold. Act now, and do it with courage and power.
- Even a mighty ruler must be selective– identify your empire and don't waste time and energy on things that aren't a priority.

- Lead from the front, get your hands dirty, and whatever you're doing, do it excellently.
- Don't overthink things. Start by conquering your own fear and hesitation.

Questions for reflection:

Am I overthinking things, and do I need to just act today, right now?

What is the single, quickest thing I can do in the next hour to smash through my procrastination, and getting moving on a stalled task?

What is crying out for my bold, hands-on action today?

Genghis Kahn

"It is not the strongest of the species that survive, nor the most intelligent, but the one most responsive to change."
- **Charles Darwin**

Unlike some of the other conquerors and heroes on our list, Genghis Kahn was born a peasant-not an aristocrat. He was born Temujin (meaning "blacksmith" or "iron") in 1162 in the Mongolian steppes, and his early life was one of desperate poverty and suffering. The word "steppe" comes from the Russian word for "grassy plain" and that is precisely what the steppes are–unbelievably vast, open grasslands inhabited by pastoral nomads who are almost more comfortable on the back of a horse than they are on foot. Each tribe was ruled over by a Kahn. To understand something of this landscape is to understand a little of the character of Genghis Kahn; the steppes were extensive, wild, open, and free–like Genghis' spirit.

Life in Mongolia 800 years ago was a brutal game of endurance. When he was just nine years of age, Genghis' father was poisoned by a rival Tatar hoard, and his own tribe abandoned his mother and her seven children to scramble for their lives. Genghis learned to hunt and forage out of sheer necessity, and the threat of starvation was imminent enough that some historians believe he even killed his brother in an argument over food.

Genghis married as a teenager and almost immediately he and his young wife were kidnapped by other rival clans and forced into slave labor before they escaped. By the time he was in his early twenties, Genghis was well-accustomed to fighting for his life, and had already won himself a reputation as a warrior and leader among his people.

He eventually gathered an army and began to forge important alliances with other surrounding clans, gradually building influence for himself, and consolidating the endlessly fractured tribes and clans under his own banner, conquest by conquest.

By the time he was 44 years old, he had done more to merge the peoples of Mongolia than any that had come before him. If the most superficial historical report is to be taken at face value, Genghis was a bloodthirsty barbarian hellbent on tearing apart the civilized world, and he and his Mongol hoard are famous for plundering their way across Asia and Europe, leaving nothing in their wake. While this is certainly part of the picture, Genghis' story is a lot more complex and interesting; the man was a great military mind, a deep thinker, and quite truly something akin to a force of nature rather than a mere man.

Genghis is known for his singular ability to learn and adapt–not just destroy. His tactic was one of appropriation: He would absorb into his own empire the very best cultural and technological remnants from the nations he committed to destruction. The Mongols were vicious and merciless, but their real violence was ideological. Granted, by other terms this is still theft and destruction all the same, but Genghis would build his own empire, on his own terms. A biographer says of him that his strategy was not aggression for its own sake, but rather "a persistent cycle of pragmatic learning, experimental adaptation, and constant revision driven by his uniquely disciplined and focused will."

From one perspective, Genghis' strategy was theft and appropriation, but we can call it something else: **learning**. From the Turks he stole the idea of organizing his troops into groups of ten soldiers–and in the process realized the value of converting the Mongols to the decimal system. From the Tangits he stole effective strategies for overcoming fortified cities. From the Chinese he stole the idea of building certain machines for destroying city walls, and from the Jurchid he stole the concept of capturing a people's heart and mind, not just their city. Though himself uneducated, once Genghis had been exposed to certain ideas in other cultures, he immediately incorporated them into his own. This kind of meta-learning was something that he was, ultimately, a master of.

As he gained more experience, Genghis travelled not only with warriors and war machines, but with translators and clerks who could interpret and intervene, allowing him to conquer on every level. He would make a practice of immediately seeking out a city's big thinkers (scribes, scholars, doctors, astrologers) and finding ways to exploit their knowledge, using their position to win hearts and minds, and taking for his own people the ideas he felt had the greatest value.

Thus, Genghis was primarily a military man, but his genius for war was swiftly converted to mastery of all other skills and resources. Genghis' army found a good use for every craftsman, cook, scientist, merchant, and scholar, and considered one of the most important spoils of war the expanding intellectual empire they would create.

In a way, Genghis' taste for war and conquest created a kingdom of interesting religious freedom and opened up trade routes and cultural exchange largely unprecedented at the time. We can thank the early Mongols for bringing the world Chinese noodles, Persian carpets, French metalwork, German technology–even Islam owes its spread to Genghis.

Today, Genghis is often considered one of the greatest conquerors of recorded history, and it's difficult to tally up his total impact, or imagine the face of the world had it not been for his "uniquely disciplined and focused will."

Learning as conquest, conquest as learning

Granted, none of us are in the position to conquer and claim literal lands for our clans, but in a sense, we all face certain intellectual domains and territories that are no less vast than the Mongolian steppes. If we consider that learning is a form of conquest, we can begin to see that Genghis has far more to teach the modern man than it may first appear.

Genghis was used to being in the wild. When you constantly encounter new and unknown situations, you cannot easily fall back on what you already know. Often, the only way to survive is to learn–and learn fast. If you can learn to swiftly manage novelty, and even turn it to your advantage, then every new situation becomes something that you can conquer and derive advantage from.

Genghis was not a scholar, but when he encountered a scholar, he quickly understood their value and put them to use towards the expansion of his own vision. Thus, he didn't *need* to be a scholar–he had conquered one. There is an interesting paradox here: it takes humility to admit the things you don't know or understand. But, it's only once you can acknowledge your state of ignorance that you can actually learn anything.

Genghis did not waste time trying to be all things. He was a warrior, and a ruler. He had one skill–learning–and from that he derived everything else. In a peculiar way, the bloodthirsty warlord Genghis was a humble man, and constantly willing to learn. He was always ready to adapt, and to ask himself of every new situation, "What do these people know that I don't? What's here that I don't yet understand?"

If we imagine the world of possible knowledge and wisdom as the vast Mongolian steppes, we can see that Genghis conquered new territory so rapidly because he was always willing to incorporate the best of everything he encountered. In particular, he could even successfully incorporate his own enemies and adversaries, and put them to use.

During a battle against the tribe Taijut, someone hit Genghis' horse with an arrow, causing it to topple. He narrowly escaped death. Later, he demanded to know who had shot the arrow, and, to his surprise, a soldier courageously claimed to have done it. Genghis noted his guts and bravery, and admired the sheer talent of the man who had made the shot. Rather than execute him, he made him an officer in his army.

In our own lives, failure, criticism, and even attack from others can serve as opportunities for learning and expansion, if we only adopt a conquering mindset, instead of a reactive, defensive one. It was precisely because he had the opportunistic attitude of a plunderer, that Genghis was able to ask of even an assassin attempt, "What good can I take from this?"

Being too secure and confident in our own knowledge and abilities is a surefire way to ensure that we stay in our comfort zone and never learn anything new. There is always the opportunity to learn, and you can learn from anything, and anyone.

From enemies and your friends.

From successes and disasters.

From the people you conquer and the people who conquer you.

At every new juncture in life, you will be exposed to something that, if you play it right, can be absorbed fruitfully into your own expanding mental "empire." The world is vast; stay a student and keep learning. Genghis Kahn was a mighty and formidable conqueror, but most of all his mind was open. Don't be defensive and inflexible. Seek to be influenced by the new things you encounter; don't assume. Absorb the world the way that Genghis absorbed the steppes.

Now, a caveat: The military history and various campaigns led by Genghis are complex and interesting. The man was estimated to have been responsible for the deaths of 40 million people (four times as many as were killed in the Holocaust), and some statistics say that he reduced the world's total population by more than 10%.

In no way would it be wise to consider the genocidal Genghis a beacon of moral behavior, nor should we hold his utilization of rape, pillaging, and murder as aspirational in any way. Rather, we are interested only in a limited feature of his attitude when it came to *how* he conquered and ruled. Reports strongly suggested that Genghis was charismatic, loyal, and humble, and we can certainly appreciate the value of these things. In fact, when considering the life of such a ruthless military commander, we can take a page out of Genghis' book and ask, "What is useful here? What can we incorporate?"

Genghis Kahn's legacy is vast and controversial, but he can teach us a lot about the nature of conquest–that it is not always about domination and imposition, but rather the willingness to conquer by absorbing, incorporating, and adoptiing every useful new thing that is encountered.

In the years after his death in Mongolia, Genghis became a national hero and was even deified, being woven into folklore and legend as a superhuman entity. His myth still survives, and so to do his genes: At the time of his death it was estimated that round 10% of all Mongol men possessed his Y chromosome, and today, it is estimated that a mind-boggling 1 in 200 men is a direct descendent of the Kahn ("The genetic legacy of the Mongols" *AJHG*, Zerjal et. al., 2003).

Look for merit, and focus on loyalty and unity

Breaking with Mongol tradition, Genghis promoted individuals based on merit rather than bloodlines. After all, he himself was not born with a title, and so he assembled his own loyal and skilled cadre of lieutenants who possessed talent and ability, their pedigree totally irrelevant.

Genghis also reorganized his forces into mixed tribal units, dissolving traditional allegiances in favor of unity under the Mongol banner. By incorporating conquered peoples into his vision and offering them a stake in his empire, he fostered long-term stability, and cultural and religious integration. This meritocratic and inclusive approach inspired loyalty and enabled him to lead one of history's most effective military forces, solidifying his legacy as both a conqueror and a unifier.

- If you're assembling a team of your own, challenge yourself to look beyond the superficial. "Hire for attitude, train for skill" as they say–or if you can, hire for attitude *and* skill, whether that attitude and skill comes from an expected source or not. This is more than mere inclusivity for its own sake; it's smart. Don't overlook people because of their background, age, gender, etc., but instead pay close attention to their ability to do the job and to adapt. Reward bravery and effort–even if it sometimes opposes you.
- Be curious about junior members, outsiders, and newcomers–they have valuable perspectives you can really learn from. If there's a new hire, for example, be curious about the position they've come from, what they know, and what fresh thinking they can bring to your workplace culture. Integrate them into the team and make room to expand and accommodate their differences, for example by asking for feedback or input on certain standard procedures or policies.
- In any group, camaraderie and cohesion will build loyalty over time. If your own family, team, or group is feeling fractured, try to find a "banner" to unify them under. What can everyone agree on? Take it upon yourself to inspire them to look past differences. For example, a Meetup group may contain

people from different generations, personality types, socioeconomic positions, and so on. Yet, if they can all agree on their love for embroidery or mountain biking or geocaching, then they can still find unity.

Be open to learning from ALL sources

Genghis Khan's openness to learning was the cornerstone of his dominance. He was not a static leader, but one who constantly absorbed ideas, technologies, and strategies from those he encountered–no matter who they were. He adopted tactics and technology from his adversaries to improve his own strategy, showing that wisdom can come from anywhere. This relentless pursuit of knowledge distinguished him from other conquerors, ensuring the Mongol Empire's resilience and long-lasting influence.

- If you want to improve a skill, seek advice not just from the experts but also from those who have only recently learned, since they can share fresh, relatable insights.
- Deliberately read books on topics you know nothing about, or material written by authors you strongly suspect you'll dislike or disagree with. Seek out social situations where you are not the most intelligent or knowledgeable or talented person in the room, but the least.

- When someone challenges you, be glad. Set your ego aside and engage with them. Could they be right? "Right" and "wrong" aside, what can this person teach you? An enemy can be a more valuable teacher than a friend. In a similar way, don't allow ego and envy to distract you from someone who you could genuinely learn from; befriend them and figure out how you too can know what they know–or at least get them on your side.
- Don't be discouraged when you don't immediately excel at something. Failure is a teacher, and provided you don't take it personally, it can show you more about yourself than easy success. If something's not working, let it go. Don't be afraid to swap it for something else, even if that thing isn't "yours." Changing and adapting is not only possible, it's usually necessary!

Leverage psychological advantage in negotiations

Genghis Khan's army was a little like the Borg in *Star Trek*–resistance really was futile, and assimilation really was the only option. But Genghis usually didn't frame things this way; instead, his offer of "surrender or destruction" gave his opponents a clear choice, steering them toward submission without wasting resources–particularly his own. In life, you can use the same sort of framing to influence outcomes without conflict.

- If you're coordinating a group trip, suggest two well-researched options rather than leaving it entirely open-ended, which can lead to indecision. Or, if you're asking a friend for help, phrase it as an opportunity for shared success: "If we do this together, we can finish much faster." Clear, confident framing often motivates others to cooperate. Then, you're united under the same banner, you're leading proactively, and you're engineering the situation on your own terms.
- In negotiations, don't think in terms of win or lose. Carefully consider what the other person is trying to achieve, and what they value, and then find a way to get them on your side so that they feel that they can still achieve their goal in a way that makes sense to them.
- During conflicts and misunderstandings, show the other parties that you are genuinely interested in their perspective, and all the things they bring to the table. When they feel valued, contributing will make them feel good, and they'll *want* to cooperate.

Elizabeth's story

Elizabeth was one of the first American importers of Japanese and Korean cosmetics. With her finger on the pulse of beauty and skincare trends, Elizabeth had quickly introduced Western consumers to exciting new brands, and soon she had built a burgeoning empire in a competitive niche known to be saturated since the 1980s.

She took frequent trip to Asia to sample the newest products, and in time developed her own hybrid brand–a tinted sunscreen of a type that had never been for sale on the American market.

One day, however, Elizabeth encountered a formidable foe: An environmental NGO took a sudden and intense interest in her new product, and began making serious claims on social media about the health safety of the ingredients in her products. They claimed that Elizabeth had failed to meet certain industry standards and was at risk of violating this and that regulation. In what appeared to be a coordinated effort, dozens of questions and complaints began to flood in. Elizabeth was terrified.

The more she looked into the matter, the more terrified she got; the environmental group boasted a seasoned chemical engineer, a food safety expert, and an expert dermatologist. Elizabeth had to admit that their criticisms were not actually unfounded: While she was a masterful businesswoman and marketer, she may have cut a few corners when it came to product development.

So, she had to think quick. Rather than get defensive or go to war with the environmental group, she arranged to meet with them privately. To their surprise, Elizabeth approached with an attitude of utter humility, and deferred at once to their superior knowledge. She asked questions. She took notes. She disarmed them by showing genuine fascination and respect for their expertise.

At the end of the meeting, Elizabeth surprised them once again: She made all three a job offer. She wanted to expand, she explained, and their knowledge and exacting standards were exactly what she would need if she intended to make a success of any further product development. She made a concerted effort to show that in this area, she would take her cue from them; they had already skillfully identified her weaknesses, and now she would ask them to help her build strength in precisely that same area. And who better to serve that role?

Two of the three accepted the offer, and within two years Elizabeth had launched more products, this time the right way. Granted, she was never on *friendly* terms with these people, but they were happy to work together on a project with the mutual aim to rid the market of unsafe cosmetics and skincare products.

Like Genghis Kahn, Elizabeth expanded her empire not by squashing detractors and adversities, but by engaging them. She neutralized her "enemy" not by destroying them, but by incorporating them. At first, she faced threat, criticism, and an outright attack; with open-mindedness and a willingness to objectively face her blind spots, she transformed those things into a (profitable) learning opportunity.

Genghis Kahn's conqueror mindset: "By learning I extend my empire."

Conqueror traits: Adaptability, resourcefulness, open-mindedness, loyalty, meritocracy, resilience.

- Always be learning. There is no situation, event, or person you cannot learn something from.
- Don't let your ego stop you from dropping what isn't working, and trying something new.
- Don't dominate, *incorporate*.
- Be humble, try new things, and keep pushing yourself out of your comfort zone.

Questions for reflection:

Thinking of my most challenging issue currently, what good can I find in it?

Might there be some talent, value, opportunity, or advantage in my situation that I'm currently not seeing?

What things in my life am I now ready to admit "I don't know"?

Empress Wu Zetian

"Remember, when onc's aim is to achieve greatness... everyone is expendable."

- **Empress Wu Zetian**

Confucius said, "A woman ruler would be as unnatural as having a hen crow like a rooster at daybreak." Empress Wu Zetian didn't merely challenge superficial gender norms in medieval China, she lived a life that was thought *impossible*. China during the Tang Dynasty was far beyond what we'd consider misogynistic today; it was not just that women were discouraged from leadership positions, but rather that the very cosmos itself was structured so that female authority and rule was as nonsensical as up becoming down, or the moon changing places with the sun.

For a period of more than 3000 years, Empress Wu Zetian was the first and only woman ever to rule China as emperor, and for that reason she is frequently added to lists of other notable female conquerors. With her exceptional intellect, political acumen, and vaulting ambition, she ruled as the "Holy and Divine Emperor" of the Second Zhou Dynasty for fifteen years. During her reign Wu implemented meritocratic reforms, elevated the role of women, and expanded the empire, cementing her legacy as a transformative yet polarizing leader. Despite the historical bias that sought to diminish her achievements, Wu's reign showcased her visionary leadership and resilience in a deeply patriarchal society.

The Empress (often called just "Wu" for short) was the daughter of a favored military strategist in the emperor's royal court, Wu Shihuo. She was born in 624 BC in Wenshui, which is now in China's Shanxi province. She was from a wealthy and privileged family, and educated in art, literature, music, and even governmental affairs–very uncommon at the time. The young girl was whip smart and ambitious, but it was her physical beauty that caught the emperor's attention, and she was quickly taken as a concubine at just 14 years of age.

Because Wu never bore the emperor any children, when he died she was expected to follow the custom of the time and live out the rest of her life as a Buddhist nun. As it happened, however, Wu again caught the eye of another powerful man, the Emperor Gaozong, heir to the throne. Historians are still undecided how this happened: Did Wu, donning a nun's robes and a shaved head, somehow capture Gaozong's heart while in the nunnery? Or–more scandalously and somewhat more believable–were the seeds of their romance planted while she still served as the prior Emperor's concubine?

Either way, Wu was spared the nunnery and instated as second concubine under Emperor Gaozong, where she swiftly won his favor. In time, she became empress herself, and bore the Emperor four sons. When the Emperor suffered a debilitating stroke, Wu was already prepared to take responsibility and handle state affairs on his behalf. Here, again, the historians are divided on exactly how this happened–did Wu lovingly step in to become de facto ruler out of duty to her beloved, or had she skillfully wrested power from him?

In any case, when he died, the eldest son and heir, Li Xian, took the throne. Almost immediately it became known that the Empress disapproved of his weak leadership and in time she had him ousted, sent away, and replaced by her younger son, Li Dan. At some point, it would have been perfectly clear to the nation and everyone in the court who was really in charge, and that no matter who happened to be *officially* in power, Wu was actually the one pulling the strings.

In time, Wu allowed her own ambition to become plainer and more obvious, and she no longer needed the façade of a male ruler to legitimize her ambitions. She usurped the throne from her own son and gave herself an illustrious title, ringing in the new Zhou dynasty, to much controversy. Like other women in our book, Wu had to work carefully to align herself with the prevailing spiritual and philosophical ideologies at the time–in her case, the central religions of Buddhism, Daoism, and Confucianism. If the popular sentiment was that women were destined for homemaking and childrearing, then she would need to style herself as something *beyond* a mere mortal woman. By aligning her image with the goddesses and other female principalities of the Buddhist faith, she would legitimize her authority and right to rule.

Had the story ended there, Wu might have been written off as merely another scheming court socialite who did whatever was necessary to secure a little power for herself. After all, many rungs on the ladder of her ascension to power had been a result of her connection to powerful men, and she had not dismantled patriarchal structures as much as struck a deal with them to her own advantage.

But Wu was not concerned with herself alone and took many unprecedented steps to reform the status of women in Chinese society. She appointed certain female officials into positions historically reserved for men, and used her influence to promote female contributions in scholarship and the arts. Wu knew very well that these appointments conferred no real power, but she understood the subtler influence of placing women in prominent and visible positions.

During her reign, she proved her competence and entitlement to her position, establishing several policies that ensured the peace and prosperity of her empire. Much like Cleopatra and Catherine the Great, however, history has often painted a cruel picture of powerful women, and her posthumous treatment by male historians has tended to exaggerate her sexual promiscuity and aggression, while stubbornly ignoring her actual achievements as a masterful leader.

Never quite shaking the "unnatural" label, Wu's story has been marred by distortions made by those who would hold no other narrative except one of the perversion of the natural order. Today, history books are filled with "great men" who are admired for their courage, ambition, and strategy, while women like Wu are relegated to soap-opera style TV series emphasizing the glitter of court life, and the lightweight titillation of harem politics.

How ruthless was Wu, in the end? It is difficult to separate out fact from fiction–bearing in mind also that certain fictions might have been deliberately cultivated for Wu's advantage. There are certainly rumors of her establishing a secret police service to continuously monitor her opposition, and she was not above torturing or executing those who threatened to rebel against her. Wu is said to have murdered her own baby in order to cast blame on the first concubine, the rival Empress Wang. The emperor believed the accusation and dismissed Wang, placing Wu in her position; Wu then had Wang executed. Legend has it that Wu ordered that the woman's hands and feet be cut off and her body thrown into a vat of wine.

What it means to be coldly calculating

Wu's ascent from concubine to empress was marked by a careful and deliberate approach to power. She overcame rivals, manipulated alliances, and secured her authority through political acumen and often ruthless tactics. Her rise demonstrated her ability to navigate a male-dominated court, using strategy to dismantle barriers that would have otherwise confined her.

What's interesting about Wu's story is how she defied certain structures and institutions using the very rules and mechanisms of those institutions themselves. Wu wasn't a radical revolutionary in the sense that we might expect of a powerful woman today; she worked *within* the confines of her male-dominated world, and dug out a place for herself using whatever was available to her.

To the modern mind, Wu's plots and antics may seem treacherous, but consider the alternative. In Wu's society, *there simply was no path* for an intelligent, capable woman to take if she desired autonomy. Thus, being coldly calculating can also be understood as pragmatism, level-headedness, and the courage to look at circumstances for what they actually are.

In many ways, Wu was the ultimate Confucian ruler, since she so skillfully adapted herself to the inevitability of her circumstances, and with serenity and tempered control she took the limits imposed on her and turned them to her advantage. Consider, for example, that Wu's first entrance into courtly life was entirely out of her control; as a young teenager she had been treated as an object of desire, a mere thing, and something for a man to possess. It was not that his will overpowered hers, but worse: that she did not have the right to a will at all. It was even likely that being selected as a concubine was considered the height of any woman's potential, and an honor.

Can you picture this series of events from a teenage girl's perspective? We cannot know if Wu resented her position, but we can tell by her actions that she did not allow it to limit her. She might have refused with indignation or defied the emperor... but she didn't. She accepted the role thrust upon her, and wrung from it every drop of gain she could.

The life of a royal concubine was one of luxurious slavery; her activities would have been severely limited, but Wu did what she could to act within those limits. Her schemes skillfully outmaneuvered her rivals, and she clawed her way to power and influence using the only avenues available to her: beauty, the ability to bear male heirs, and the favor of the emperor. Once she had elevated herself within these confines, Wu dropped them and used other men–this time her own sons–to further leverage power. Like Catherine the Great, she worked with what she had. It was not her game, certainly, but she would play by the rules and win it anyway. Under her name, Tang rule was consolidated, and the empire strengthened and unified.

Towards the end of her life, the notorious Zhang brothers won the Empress's affections through flattery that was roundly resented by other courtiers and senior officials. Though the Emperess was warned to avoid the Zhangs, she failed to distance herself. Finally, after a well-orchestrated conspiracy against her, the palace was seized by generals and ministers who immediately executed the Zhang brothers and forced the Empress to abdicate, which she did given her poor health. She retired to another palace and died later that year, at the age of 81.

Turn adversity into a stepping stone

Wu's life began in obscurity as a concubine, but she leveraged her intelligence and ambition to rise far above her station. She achieved what she did not because she broke free of a suffocating system that constricted her freedom, but because she **leveraged that system to her own ends.**

Consider that a concubine had fewer rights than a legal wife, yet was expected to produce heirs for the emperor, all while being forbidden any other relations. Concubines were ranked and so were their children. Though they did live in some material comfort, they were essentially bought as slaves and could be divorced at will. Concubinage was fundamentally prostitution, and widowed concubines could be killed and buried with their husbands or shipped off to nunneries.

Circumstances of this kind could easily be considered an impediment for a woman of intelligence, talent, and ambition. Wu, however, used it as an opportunity for growth. If she must survive inside a world of harem intrigue, competing with other women, then at least let her win. If the only way out of that system was to be promoted to the status of a wife, then that's what she would do.

Consider also the story about the death of Wu's baby. It may have been that she did indeed murder the child in order to depose the first concubine, but the other option is also intriguing; perhaps Wu's baby simply died, and she saw in it an opportunity. While a grisly story either way, we cannot help but see the power of turning adversity to your advantage.

- When faced with setbacks, focus on how they can serve as opportunities for growth. For instance, if you're overlooked for a promotion, take the chance to acquire new skills or build connections that position you better for the next opportunity. Like Wu, use adversity as a launchpad.
- Keep looking ahead at how situations might evolve so that you can position yourself advantageously. Anticipate challenges and obstacles and find ways that you can *frame yourself as part of the solution,* thus making yourself indispensable. For example, pay attention to the things your superiors are struggling with in the workplace, and learn how to solve their problems for them. You will instantly win favor–while furnishing yourself with skills that will always be useful.
- If you fail, make a mistake, or cause offense, set aside your fear and ego and think of ways to swiftly use the situation to your benefit. For example, if you've made a costly mistake at work, immediately own up to it and offer a carefully considered plan to mitigate the damage and make things right. Your mistake will still be a mistake, but you will have also

seized an opportunity to demonstrate your honesty, your responsibility, and your initiative. The impression you create after a setback may last longer than the consequences of the setback itself.

Champion merit in your sphere

During Wu's 45-year reign, China quickly became a superpower. The economy was revitalized and government corruption was curtailed. Like Genghis Kahn, the Empress surrounded herself with those she considered competent and skillful, with much less regard for their social standing than was the norm in Imperial China at the time. She reformed the imperial examination system for the election of officials, for example, so that it selected for ability, not family connections. The result was not just admiration and increasing public popularity, but a more efficient and effective meritocracy.

Wu herself was not considered from a high enough ranking family to deserve the seat of Empress, and yet she attained it. She was so opposed to the question of China being ruled by incompetent monarchs that she even despised that incompetence in her own sons–although, true to form, this was another adversity that she fully exploited to her advantage.

- Wu's reforms in governance show the power of recognizing talent over privilege. In your own life, whether you're leading a team or mentoring someone, prioritize ability and effort over status or connections. For example, if you're organizing a project, choose collaborators based on people's enthusiasm and skills, not just their seniority or familiarity. This strengthens outcomes and builds trust and fairness.

- Wu's dynasty was known for being a relatively prosperous, peaceful, and stable time in Chinese history. Compared to the intrigue and high drama of her own life, she ruled with quiet magnanimity. Whether in your private or professional life, take the time to notice, acknowledge, and reward competence when you see it. If you manage a team, go out of your way to recognize and incentivize good work, no matter who it's coming from. By the same token, guard against automatically approving of something just because it comes from someone you already like; be objective.
- Never be tempted to rest on your laurels. Wu was well-educated, but stayed a life-long student and continually read on a wide range of subjects, from calligraphy and art to history and politics. Her reign was not merely about personal ambition; she governed her homeland with shrewdness and intellect. When it came to merit, she reserved the strictest standards for herself.

Challenge norms with quiet strength

Wu reshaped traditional roles, not by overt rebellion but through calculated actions that proved her capabilities over time. She was not a flash in the pan or a mere figurehead for women's empowerment, but a genuinely skilled ruler. **Wu was a woman, but this was not her sole or most important characteristic**. She was intelligent, articulate, well-educated, and had a knack for leadership–and her ambition meant she would not allow gender norms to restrict her. Thus, she did not demand special accommodations from others, nor ask permission for the right to rule–she simply got on with doing what she wanted to do.

- When confronting systemic biases—be it at work, school, or in your community—focus on demonstrating competence and advocating for change subtly yet persistently. For example, if you notice unequal opportunities in your workplace, propose solutions or mentorship programs that address the imbalance without alienating others.
- Wu conquered the Forbidden City from the inside out, and she did it without an army. Try not to be discouraged by long-established hierarchies that exclude you. Instead, figure out what you *can* do, and how you can make the best of the opportunities that are available–then build on that. For

example, you may be a woman in a competitive male-dominated industry, but if you can make just one or two allies, you can over time leverage that to your own ends.
- Be patient. Wu was well into her sixties when she finally attained the throne and had been slowly gathering influence over *decades* since she had entered the court at just 14. She did not become Empress overnight, but by a long, slow succession of carefully plotted steps. Concerning your own goals, try not to overwhelm yourself by thinking how far you must go, and instead just keep your eyes focused on the next move in front of you.

Aidan's story

Though Aidan grew up in inner city Manchester, UK–an area notorious for high teen pregnancy rates and gun crime–he was lucky to have a mother who was hellbent on placing him in a school where he might have better opportunities. But this came with a major downside: Being of Jamaican descent, Aidan was one of the few non-white students in his class. A born and bred Mancunian, Aidan nevertheless felt like an outsider. Despite occasional bullying and exclusion, however, he graduated near the top of his class and looked set to begin the career he dreamed of as a boy.

But it was in the professional world that Aidan began to really understand the meaning of the term "institutional racism." Newly recruited to a prestigious firm in London, Aidan was quickly discouraged by the subtle (and not-so-subtle) attitude of some of his coworkers. Some would sneeringly ask if he could hook them up with cannabis, others would slyly suggest he had been hired purely to fulfil DEI requirements. When he pushed back and stood up for himself or other marginalized groups, he was accused of being "angry" and intimidating others. A year in, he was passed over for a promotion, and the role Aidan had been angling for for months was given to a new hire instead.

Aidan pushed on, but felt increasingly demoralized and trapped. One day, a fellow colleague made a horrific accusation: He claimed that Aidan had stolen money from his desk. Over the course of the next few months, Aidan's world descended into chaos as he tried to prepare for a messy employment tribunal to determine whether the accusation had been an instance of racial discrimination.

Throughout it all, however, Aidan tried to keep his head. Despite being around people who had it out for him, he kept his feelings of rage and injustice under wraps and got to work learning everything he could about the process. He gathered evidence, he studied up on the law, and–crucially–he began to form strategic alliances with key members in his team, particularly his direct supervisor, who had felt some sympathy for his situation.

While his friends encouraged him to resign and cut his losses, Aidan dug his heels in. He was used to doing twice as much to earn half as much recognition, and now, his diligence and knowledge was starting to pay dividends. By continually defending against every accusation with factual evidence and calm logic and reason, Aidan slowly established himself as someone who would quietly hold his ground. Increasingly, the colleague's accusation began to look more and more unfounded and petty–and from the company's perspective, *expensive*.

By the time the tribunal ruled in Aidan's favor, he had completely shifted public perception. There was no decisive blow that won the victory; rather, it was quiet determination and stamina to persistently "play the game," even though the rules had been set against him. Over time, Aidan's enemy revealed themselves to be a company liability, while Aidan took the opportunity to quietly showcase his value.

Within five years, he had won the begrudging respect of others who could no longer deny his work ethic and value to the company. In ten years, the tribunal was a distant memory. However, Aidan would never forget it. He believed that the event had been one of the most fortunate and formative of his career. Why? Because it had shown him, and others, what he was capable of. He had lived his life under prejudice, but that episode had taught him that he was far from powerless in fighting it. He had conquered not just other people's prejudices, but his own fear and self-doubt.

In his field, Aidan would eventually be recognized as a supremely trustworthy and fair player, and his commitment to equality and merit inspired and reassured many, even those who initially underestimated him. Aidan had always stood out; now, he was still standing out, but on his own terms.

It took time, but he had the last word. He refused to see himself as a victim, and he used his own persecution as a means to build himself up. Was racism still an everyday problem? Sadly, yes. But he kept in mind the words of John Henrik Clarke: "To hold a people in oppression you have to convince them first that they are supposed to be oppressed." Aidan was able to conquer when he realized that he would never, *ever* agree that he was supposed to be oppressed.

Like Empress Wu, he simply would not agree with other people's assessment of his abilities and potential; *he* would decide what his life would be, and he would use everything–adversity included–to help him get there.

Empress Wu Zetian's conqueror mindset: "Every adversity, every failure, every heartache carries with it the seed of an equal or greater benefit."

Conqueror traits: Resilience, level-headedness, resourcefulness, fairness, quiet strength, patient persistence.

- When faced with setbacks, focus on how they can serve as opportunities for growth.
- No matter what, hold yourself to your own standards and be a champion for real merit, even if others aren't.
- Be patient, persistent, and assured in your own quiet strength.
- Don't argue with prejudice. Don't wait for other people's permission to go against norms. Just do it. Be the change.

Julius Caesar

"Cowards die many times before their deaths,
The valiant never taste of death but once.
Of all the wonders that I yet have heard,
It seems to me most strange that men should fear,
Seeing that death, a necessary end,
Will come when it will come."

- **Caesar in Shakespeare's play *Julius Caesar*, Act 2 Scene 2.**

Born in 100 BC, Julius Caesar remains one of history's most iconic and recognizable leaders. A much-lauded Roman general and statesman, Caesar conquered Gaul (modern-day France), expanded the Roman Republic's territories, and reformed Rome into a more centralized state. After a victorious campaign against his rival Pompey in a civil war, he declared himself dictator in 49 BC. Over the course of his life he led some twenty battles, being defeated in just three of them.

Although his sweeping reforms modernized Rome, his consolidation of power created bitter enemies among the Senate. His assassination on the Ides of March marked the end of the Roman Republic and ushered in the Roman Empire. Caesar's legacy remains with us still, and his rule was instrumental in establishing the Roman Empire.

Caesar has become so much of an emblem that it's difficult to imagine what he, the human being, was really like. We can look to his ascent into power, his ambitious alliances, his victories, even his assassination… but can we see beyond all this to the character beneath?

Caesar was known in his time to be charismatic and sociable. Early in life he gained a reputation for boldness, strategy, and a high tolerance for risk and uncertainty–in other words, confidence. But to understand more about Caesar, we need to know about the culture that created him.

In ancient Rome, there existed a concept called *virtus*, which comes from the early Latin root for "man" and also gives us words like "virile" and "virtue." The concept of virtus encompassed a range of qualities and characteristics belonging to the ideal male, most usually emperors, kings, and rulers. To possess virtus was to be boldly masculine, courageous, wise, strong, and of well-disciplined physical prowess.

Much of the modern Western world owes its image of the heroic warrior to this early Roman ideal. Before the enlightenment, aristocratic men of excellence were expected to possess a full set of qualities: practical wisdom, a noble sense of justice, courage, self-control and discipline, plus temperance and moderation.

Connected to this character was an expectation around ideal action and right conduct; that is, an excellent man (if he wished to be fit for leadership) should have a robust work ethic, a sound intellect, and a track record of upright civic conduct. Though the ideal eventually changed, at the time of Caesar's reign a man would be thought unmanly if he did not at some point serve in the military, if he could not speak well, if he lacked education, or if he was morally crooked.

Enter Caesar, a young man who from his youth manifested all these qualities to an impressive extreme. Though other notable historical figures have been included on our list because of some special defining quality, we cannot strictly take this approach with Caesar, since he had no single defining quality–**his effectiveness came instead from his *virtus*, that is, his complete cohesion and maturity as a well-rounded and excellent person.**

For those who are interested in Caesar's military resume or the biographical details of his life, there is such a wealth of insightful commentary available today that we need not spend time rehashing it here. He was elected as consul in 60 BC and formed an alliance with Crassus and Pompey, creating what was called the First Triumvirate, with Caesar commanding four legions. With these legions and remarkable military prowess and skill, he conquered Gaul. Though he did eventually reign as Rome's dictator, his rivals orchestrated a coup that saw him assassinated within a year. When he was stabbed to death in 44 BC by rebel senators led by Brutus and Cassius, the Roman Republic fell with him.

The virtue of calculated boldness

So what precisely made Caesar such a renowned hero and conqueror? It was not just bravery or charisma or cunning or intelligence, but rather the way that *all* these attributes came together to form a whole. Julius Caesar was the full package, and his power came from being *balanced*.

If we consider aesthetic and artistic expression from the era, we will see that the ideal Roman man was physically fit, strong, and muscular, and that the model face was considered one of classical lines, elegance, and *proportion*. Such an appearance, the ancient Romans believed, reflected an upright and correct manner of living–one that was just as graceful, refined, and proportionate, and which didn't veer to either extreme.

This is a visual metaphor of certain inner qualities; Caesar was fearless and courageous, but he knew how to temper this with restraint and caution when necessary. He was audacious and confident when necessary, but he knew exactly when to be prudent, and when to hold his tongue. He was an ardent and willful soul, yet a true Roman, he refused to be enslaved by his own passions, and would rule over himself with discipline and temperance.

In battle, it was his *calculated boldness* that characterized his rise to power–this balanced mix of virtues. His willingness to take daring yet deliberate risks set him apart from his contemporaries. On the battlefield, his unconventional blend of boldness and careful planning not only secured his military victories but also allowed him to reshape Rome's political landscape, cementing his legacy as a transformative figure in history.

Consider for example the Crossing of the Rubicon in 49 BC. Caesar's approach to this event was so singular that today we use the phrase as an idiom that roughly means "committing fully to a risky course of action."

Now, The Rubicon at the time was a shallow river that lay at the border between Italy and

Cisalpine Gaul. Roman governors were not allowed to enter the home province without an invitation from the senate. This rule existed to prevent governors, who had their own armies, from bringing military forces into Rome without authorization. In crossing this river with his army, Caesar was defying a Senate order and effectively declaring war. But in crossing, Caesar also forced Pompey and many of the ruling consuls and leaders to beat a hasty retreat out of Rome. During the ensuing Battle of Pharsalus, Caesar defeated Spain and eventually rose to become dictator of Rome.

Today, military historians see this move as one of audacity and impressive risk-taking, and yet for Caesar it was not something rash or reckless. It was planned and fully controlled. He is recorded as saying once, "If you must break the law, do it to seize power: in all other cases, observe it." And this exemplifies the precise attitude that made Caesar the powerhouse he was–even his law-breaking gall was purposeful and strategic. His risk paid off and he did in fact seize power.

Redefine the rules with purpose

Bring this boldness into your own life by carefully rethinking norms. Too often, we are encouraged by motivational speakers and self-help gurus to be outrageously confident in ourselves, to be brave, and to throw ourselves into our plans with fearless resolve. While this is an admirable quality to cultivate, it's not the full story; blind confidence is often indistinguishable from foolishness.

We need to think carefully about what we are going to put our faith in, when, why, and how. We need to *calculate* those risks and opportunities, be rational and objective about the best paths available to us, and *then* be brave and insistent as we take inspired action. But we cannot take that inspired action unless we are informed by a sound strategy first. In this sense, we must let our heads rule our hearts, and not the other way around.

Thus, it is not whether we do or do not follow the rules, but rather the extent to which we are taking active responsibility for our ambitions, setting goals, and doing something to achieve those goals, to the best of our abilities. Caesar's mindset was one of natural, dominant leadership; to him, the fact that crossing the Rubicon was illegal was neither here nor there. However, he was not just a rebel who broke rules for no other reason than to break them; had it been strategically to his advantage to follow the rules, then that is what he would have done.

Conquerors possess the willingness to be their own authority. This is what allows them to lead in the first place; they are willing to forge new paths and try something else, even something risky. Leaders like Caesar have, since the dawn of history, changed humanity in precisely this way–by sheer audacity.

- Don't worry so much about the rules all the time. Of course, there's no point creating trouble for yourself or others, but think carefully about those instances where the rules are really just tired habits and conventions. Strategically push against them. If you encounter a roadblock or obstacle, ask yourself, "Is it really true that I can't do this?" Then allow yourself to imagine what might happen if you did cross that boundary, metaphorically speaking. While some would consider it a moral grey area, for instance, there are some situations where it might be "better to ask for forgiveness than permission." Sometimes, rule-breaking is worth the gain. Don't accept no for an answer until you've made that calculation!
- If a personal goal seems out of reach, switch strategies-perhaps abandoning a rigid routine for something creative and experimental. Just as Caesar's actions had intent, ensure your bold moves are deliberate and meaningful. Occasionally, the rules we need to break are just our own limited expectations for how we can go about achieving our ends. When we let go of those rules we see that we are capable of a lot more than we originally thought.
- Use the element of surprise to your advantage. Occasionally, you can gain an

edge simply by taking a step that others would never expect, or one that they are too cautious to take themselves. Make the first move. While others are trying to figure out what just happened, you are boldly going ahead and making it happen. At work, instigate a new project, make an unexpected request, or be the first to try something a little risky.

Make your words stick

Caesar's mastery of communication set him apart as a leader. A gifted orator and writer, Caesar excelled at conveying his ideas with clarity and precision. His ability to articulate his goals inspired confidence and rallied support, both on and off the battlefield.

Being a masterful orator was also a part of the necessary skillset for an accomplished Roman statesman. It was not enough to be good, strong, and brave; one had to know how to effectively persuade and inspire, to hold one's own in conversation, to have wit and to speak with logic, reason, and clarity. The ancient Romans placed enormous emphasis on rhetoric and saw governance as a natural extension of an individual's linguistic and philosophical prowess.

- Be artful and strategic in the way you speak. *Everything* you say has the chance to be persuasive, and allow you to shape the narrative. Imagine you're convincing your friends to take an impromptu road trip. Instead of saying, "Let's go for a drive," try, "Let's hit the road and make stories we'll laugh about for years." Use targeted language that speaks to people's needs and emotions. Wield language like a tool.

- Learn how to articulate. If you're not a naturally verbal person, then know that you can learn–commit to studying a new vocabulary word every day, read the classics, or take up public speaking or debate as a hobby. You may find that singing, acting, or improv classes help you acquire more confident and controlled delivery.
- Brevity is the soul of wit. After the war with Pharnacles II of Pontus, Caesar was required to create a detailed report of the conquest, and wrote merely, "I came, I saw, I conquered." The phrase proved so catchy–especially in its original language–that it still resonates today. To do the same, be the kind of person who means what he says and says what he means; speak plainly to show confidence. Be sincere and forthright. According to Oliver Wendell Holmes, "Speak clearly, if you speak at all; carve every word before you let it fall."

Cultivate strategic presence in every encounter

Caesar was born into a patrician (ruling elite) family and his pedigree meant he always conducted himself appropriately. He was educated as an aristocrat and had as a lover none other than Queen Cleopatra of Egypt. Caesar held his head extraordinarily high.

Julius Caesar had an unparalleled knack for ensuring every moment worked to his advantage. Whether debating in the Senate, addressing a crowd, or even dining with allies, he made each encounter meaningful and memorable. As a conqueror, then, his way was to **conquer every moment**, to stand tall and to hold himself with an attitude of self-possession. He dressed well, he spoke well, and he commanded attention.

We can take a page from Caesar's book even though the golden era of mythical military heroes is long past:

- No matter who you are or what you are trying to achieve, approach every interaction–even causal ones–with intention. For example, if you're chatting with a neighbor at a barbecue, subtly mention an exciting project you're working on or a unique skill you've been honing. Plan ahead if possible. These moments can organically spark opportunities, expand

your influence, or attract allies who align with your broader ambitions. Don't be passive and let events run away with you; grab ahold of them and proactively decide what *you* want to do with them.
- Stay present in the moment. Pay attention to your posture, your gestures, and your facial expressions. All of us communicate plenty before we even open our mouths. It may feel silly at first, but before entering any new situation, try to imagine how an admired role model might conduct themselves. An alternative is to have a few affirmations, visualizations, or phrases you recite before any encounter, to remind you of your values and goals, and give you courage to hold your own.
- One excellent way to give your speech and demeanor more gravity is to simply refrain from saying "um" or "like" in your speech. Instead, just pause. Don't rush and take the time to breathe properly so that you articulate your speech clearly. A well-timed pause here and there will convey a stronger sense of presence, self-mastery, and confidence. Try it.

Terry's story

Terry is a seasoned hiring manager who, over the course of a decades-long career, has learned how to select for people who will go above and beyond the job description. In Terry's field, it's not enough to have the qualifications and the experience; what ultimately makes the difference is a certain character-and that character can be difficult to discern.

Nevertheless, Terry has devised several methods for identifying just the right personality. Of course, he reviews the applications and filters out the best candidates in all the usual ways, but to home in on just one candidate from his shortlist, he takes a different approach.

Before every interview, he sets up the interview room in a particular way:

He sets out two chairs for the candidate to sit on; one that is extremely uncomfortable and too low, and the other that is ideal.

He leaves a pen lying casually on the floor near the chairs.

He arranges for someone to casually walk into the room mid-interview, apologize, then leave without closing the door behind them.

Terry sets things up this way for a reason. He waits to see if the candidate notices the pen on the floor, and especially if they pick it up and place it back on the table. He deliberately seats the candidate in the uncomfortable chair, and watches to see if they get up and seat themselves in the other chair. Finally, he pays close attention to how the candidate responds to the interruption. Do they close the door again?

These things might seem minor, but Terry has earned that the way candidates respond to these three small details tells him a lot about their overall willingness to take calm, confident control of a situation. Do they possess enough initiative to pick the pen up, even though there's nothing in it for them? Such is a person who will see that something isn't working, and will step in to fix it, rather than passively believe that "it's someone else's job."

Likewise, a candidate who gets up and moves to the better chair is showing an ability to "break the rules" in a tiny but reasonable way. This is a person who is self-assured and willing to take steps to improve their own situation, without waiting for guidance or permission. They are a problem-solver. Finally, though anyone can prepare for an interview, the candidate's will not have prepared for an unexpected interruption. Terry watches their response, and whether they again take the initiative to re-claim ownership of the space afterwards by getting up to close the door again.

What Terry is really trying to observe is not the actions the candidates do or do not take, but rather the attitude they bring to a new and somewhat unknown situation. Are they comfortable holding their own and standing their ground? Do they take the initiative rather than wait for prompting? Do they possess their own gravitas? These things are difficult to determine by simply reading resumes.

What Terry's method reveals is that real leadership, and a true conqueror mindset, is 100% about attitude. It's about the orientation of your attention, your sense of self-mastery, and your willingness to shape the world to your ends, rather than reactively be shaped by it. This is a subtle but decisive character trait–and one that is well worth refining and cultivating in yourself. The next time you notice yourself feeling willing to trust, respect, and follow someone, pay attention and you may get a glimpse of this quality at work.

Julius Caesar's conqueror mindset: "Self-control is strength. Right thought is mastery. Calmness is power. What stands in my way becomes my way."

Conqueror traits: Bold but calculated audacity, confidence, presence, fearlessness, eloquence, dignity, and poise.

- Set your own terms, be strategic and do not be afraid of taking bold action, even if it breaks the rules.
- Take control of your presence in every encounter, and be deliberate in your expression.
- Master language and learn to use words with clarity and persuasion.

- Own the situation. Go first, try something new, and stand tall in your own initiative.

Questions for reflection:

Is there some initiative I've been avoiding taking in my life?

If I were to be boldly calculating right now, what would I lose? And what would I gain?

Being honest, what areas of my own presence and presentation need a little work?

www.ingramcontent.com/pod-product-compliance
Lightning Source LLC
Chambersburg PA
CBHW060606080526
44585CB00013B/702